The
Suppressed History
of American
Banking

"Very smart people always say if you want to discover the truth about almost anything, 'follow the money!' Well, if you want to discover some truth about money in America, read Xaviant Haze's *The Suppressed History of American Banking*!"

JOHN BARBOUR, ACTOR, COMEDIAN,
TELEVISION HOST, AND WRITER AND
DIRECTOR OF THE DOCUMENTARY FILM
THE JFK ASSASSINATION: THE JIM GARRISON TAPES

"Excellent history and research by Xaviant Haze. It is rare to find someone who takes the time to discover true history. This book puts so much into perspective. I am grateful to Xaviant for bringing all of this information to public knowledge."

STEWART A. SWERDLOW, COFOUNDER OF EXPANSIONS.COM,
RESEARCHER, LECTURER, AND AUTHOR OF *TRUE WORLD
HISTORY: HUMANITY'S SAGA* AND *BLUE BLOOD, TRUE BLOOD*

The
Suppressed History
of American
Banking

How Big Banks Fought Jackson,
Killed Lincoln,
and Caused the Civil War

XAVIANT HAZE

Bear & Company
Rochester, Vermont • Toronto, Canada

Bear & Company
One Park Street
Rochester, Vermont 05767
www.BearandCompanyBooks.com

Text stock is SFI certified

Bear & Company is a division of Inner Traditions International

Library of Congress Cataloging-in-Publication Data
Names: Haze, Xaviant, author.
Title: The suppressed history of American banking : how big banks fought
   Jackson, killed Lincoln, and caused the Civil War / Xaviant Haze.
Description: Rochester, Vermont : Bear & Company , [2016] | Includes
   bibliographical references and index.
Identifiers: LCCN 2016003643 | ISBN 9781591432333 (paperback)
   | ISBN 9781591432340 (e-book)
Subjects: LCSH: Banks and banking—Political aspects—United
   States—History—19th century. | Federal Reserve Banks—History—19th
   century. | United States—History—1783–1865. | Rothschild family. |
   Bankers—Political activity—United States—History—19th century. |
   BISAC: BODY, MIND & SPIRIT / Mythical Civilizations. | HISTORY /
   United States / Civil War Period (1850–1877).
Classification: LCC HG2472 .H39 2016 | DDC 332.10973—dc23
LC record available at http://lccn.loc.gov/2016003643

Printed and bound in the United States by Lake Book Manufacturing, Inc.
The text stock is SFI certified. The Sustainable Forestry Initiative® program
promotes sustainable forest management.

10 9 8 7 6 5 4 3 2 1

Text design and layout by Virginia Scott Bowman
This book was typeset in Garamond Premier Pro with Minion Pro used as the
   display typeface

Artwork is in the public domain unless otherwise stated.

To send correspondence to the author of this book, mail a first-class letter to the
author c/o Inner Traditions • Bear & Company, One Park Street, Rochester, VT
05767, and we will forward the communication, or contact the author directly at
www.xaviantvision.com.

★★★

This book is dedicated to my American ancestors and
to the explorers of the past, present, and future.
And to the Blackfeet Indians . . .

Contents

★★★

1

The Forgotten War of 1812

The Wild Honeysuckle

Fair flower, that dost so comely grow
Hid in this silent, dull retreat
Untouched thy honied blossoms blow
Unseen thy little branches greet
. . . No roving foot shall crush thee here
. . . No busy hand provoke a tear
By Nature's self in white arrayed
She bade thee shun the vulgar eye
And planted here the guardian shade
And sent soft waters murmuring by
. . . Thus quietly thy summer goes
. . . Thy days declining to repose
Smit with those charms, that must decay
I grieve to see your future doom
They died—nor were those flowers more gay
The flowers that did in Eden bloom
. . . Unpitying frosts, and Autumn's power
. . . Shall leave no vestige of this flower
From morning suns and evening dews
At first thy little being came
If nothing once, you nothing lose
For when you die you are the same

> *. . . The space between, is but an hour*
> *. . . The frail duration of a flower*
> PHILLIP FRENEAU (1786)

> *The tree of liberty must be refreshed from time to time*
> *with the blood of patriots and tyrants.*
> THOMAS JEFFERSON

The trouble with history is that none of us alive today were there to see what happened, and if the truth is written by the winners then it can easily be distorted in time by the losers. Comprised as it is with competing political agendas, various belief systems, and myriad patterns of tradition, history has been shown to be little more than "his-story." Seldom, if ever, is it "her-story" either. The decades after the American Revolution were tense, and although it was believed that America won the war, it might not have been as clear-cut a victory as has been taught in history class.

As Americans we learn that our freedom stems from the Declaration of Independence, which was fortified by winning the Revolutionary War. The Declaration of Independence was inspired by the eight-hundred-year-old Magna Carta, which Thomas Jefferson looked to when summoning the courage to write about breaking free from tyrannical King George III. The Magna Carta, authorized in 1215 by the king of England, was a turning point in guaranteeing individual human rights and establishing the idea that nobody, not even a king, is above the law. While the Magna Carta and its wayward son the Declaration of Independence are familiar to most English-speaking people, rarely is there any talk of the other signed treaties and charters between Britain and the United States that date back to the 1600s.

One in particular is the First Charter of Virginia of 1606, signed by King James I. (This is the same King James who edited the Bible that most Americans now read.) This charter granted the British forefathers of America a license to colonize and settle lands while guaranteeing that the future kings and queens of England would maintain sovereign authority over all of our country's citizens. This document was strengthened by the establishment of a corporation called the Virginia Company. This company, formed by King James, acquired most of the known land in America and secured the rights to 50 percent of all gold and silver mined on it, as well as percentages from other profitable ventures that colonists of the time might initiate and develop. The lands owned by the Virginia Company were leased to the colonies, and all essential and future benefits from these lands were retained by the English crown.

The crown's laws were derived from Roman laws, and the monarchs of England were nothing more than puppets whose strings were being pulled from deep within the Vatican. The common laws of England are basically extensions of Roman municipal laws—essentially Roman civil decrees designed to control insolvent states and keep a steady stream of tax money flowing to the emperor. With the implementation of the feudal system in England it became clear that all of its people were now slaves of the crown, and by 1302 Pope Boniface VIII's papal bull *Unam Sanctam* declared "that every human creature be subject to the Roman pontiff." Thus were English-speaking subjects (i.e., slaves) governed under ancient Roman laws, which included laws of the sea. Our incorporated bodies are nothing more than make-believe ships sailing the imaginary waters.

In support of this conceptual association, contemplate for a moment the number of maritime words and terms in common use today. Words like "sale/sail"—or how about after being born we are given a "birth/berth certificate"? The "berth" in nautical terms is a location in a port or harbor where a ship is moored when not at sea. This mooring naturally leads to the "dock," and it's the "doctor" who signs your "birth/berth certificate." A ship's captain also has to produce a "berth certificate" after berthing his ship at the dock. When we are born, we flood through our mother's "birth/berth canal" in a pool of water. And to those who have at one time or another ended up in court, your case files are placed in a "docket."

As we all know, going to court is expensive and requires a lot of money—and money, according to Roman law, is symbolized by water. And if I were to ask you "Where is the bank?" would you point me to the nearest Citibank down the street or tell me that it's on both sides of a river, given that riverbanks—"banks"—are controlled by currents—"currency"—and also by the flowing of water—"money."

When someone loses his home we say that his house is "under water." When financial burdens become too much, we find ourselves "drowning" in debt. Money troubles often lead to desperate actions that can land you in jail, and once in jail you look for someone to "bail you out." In the 1400s the verb "bail" meant to bucket water out of a boat. "Boat" is an old Germanic word for the more modern word "ship." The definition of a ship is "a large vessel for transporting people or goods by sea."

Some of our modern, familiar words that have the word "ship" in them include the following:

apprenticeship	lordship
censorship	ownership
citizenship	partnership
dealership	relationship
fellowship	scholarship
friendship	township
leadership	worship

According to alternative historians like Jordan Maxwell the maritime law of the ocean is international. In addition, every person born in the United States is a "ship" who is given a social security number that is registered on the New York Stock Exchange, thus granting them "citizenship." Now branded numerically, each American human being

Fig. 1.1. *Surrender of Lord Cornwallis* by John Trumbull (1820),
Rotunda of the United States Capitol

thus becomes an economic entity in the capitalistic system that defines the American system.

Whether or not these archaic laws and their hidden connections to the English crown are still relevant is fun to ponder, especially when considering that after the Revolutionary War, King George III still received payments for his corporate business venture of colonizing America.

When England lost the war the king had to relinquish most of his control over the American colonies, but because of the 1606 Virginia charter he would continue to be paid under the table while publicly fighting for war reparations. The crown cleverly used the 1783 Treaty of Paris to formally recognize America's independence while plotting their next moves behind the scenes. It is interesting to note that in the treaty's first paragraph the king not only refers to himself as the prince of the United States but also as the prince of the Holy Roman Empire! Did the American signers of this treaty, including Benjamin Franklin, John Jay, and John Adams, strengthen the granted privileges of the king of England?

These three negotiators and signers of the treaty were all esquires. An esquire was a title of dignity and trust granted by the king. It also indicated that the person bearing the title was a lawyer. Benjamin Franklin, the main negotiator of the terms of the Treaty of Paris, spent most of the war traveling between the brothels of England and France. His use of the title esquire was a tacit oath of loyalty to the British crown.

Two years after the war and bloody battles had ended, King George's treaty would officially grant the colonies their independence. In the treaty's fourth article, however, the United States agreed to pay back all bona fide debts to the king. These debts, plus the continued gold, silver, and copper payments due the crown from the Virginia Company, would ensure that the grasp of the English monarchy over the American colonies was never entirely relinquished.

When Cornwallis surrendered his sword to Washington at Yorktown he may have lost the war, but he had won the battle of attrition. Too cowardly to bring the sword to Washington himself, he had a servant deliver it along with a chilling statement concerning the future of America. According to the book *Legions of Satan*, written in 1781, Cornwallis told Washington that "a holy war will now begin on America, and when it is ended America will be supposedly the citadel of freedom, but her millions will unknowingly be loyal subjects to the Crown . . . in less than two hundred years the whole nation will be working for divine world government. That government that they believe to be divine will be the British Empire. All religion will be permeated with Judaism without even being noticed by the masses and they will all be under the invisible All-seeing Eye of the Grand Architect of Freemasonry."[1]

The author of this book, Jonathan Williams, was a West Point

Fig. 1.2. *King George III* by Allan Ramsay (1762),
National Portrait Gallery, London

graduate and grandnephew of Benjamin Franklin, a friend of Thomas Jefferson, and was even elected to Congress before his death in 1815. His writings were extensive, and a mass volume of his library still exists; however, his book *Legions of Satan,* claiming that Cornwallis prophesied the downfall of America to George Washington, has literally disappeared off the face of the Earth. That is, if it ever existed at all! The first mention of it comes from a 1994 blog post, and even a relentless search of antiquarian bookstores has yet to reveal a verifiable copy.

All that the Paris treaty of 1783 really did was to remove America as a liability of the king, who now no longer needed to financially support his western subjects. At the same time, the king was planning—with the banking wizards of his day—to infiltrate the banking system of the newly established country. The king knew that more prolonged physical wars would do more harm than good, and with the constant and ongoing struggle for European supremacy with France, his empire was teetering on the brink of destruction. The king decided to fight a new war without Americans ever being aware they were in one. This would be a banking war fought with a cunning cast of key figures placed in perfect positions to get the job done. This would be easy for the crown given that relations with America hadn't really improved after the Revolution.

The British had flooded the market with their goods and imposed trade restrictions and tariffs that prevented Americans from exporting their goods. The British still even had forts manned with soldiers in areas west of Pennsylvania that they refused to abandon, yet should have according to the Treaty of Paris. Thirteen years after America supposedly won the war, the British still maintained these armed forts in the country while its navy constantly seized and kidnapped American goods and sailors, impressing these freemen as servants of the crown and its Royal Navy. The British naval practice of forcing men into service via impressment was a common one that dated back to the medieval era. As the Mariner's Museum explains:

Under British law, the navy had the right, during time of war, to sweep through the streets of Great Britain, essentially arresting men and placing them in the Royal Navy. Naval press gangs operated throughout England in organized districts overseen by naval captains. When there was a need for new recruits the gangs would move through the waterfront districts searching for "Roderick Random," as they called the men they pressed. Under law, the press gangs could take almost anyone they happened to find. However, some individuals were protected from the press: apprentices already indentured to a master, seamen with less than two years' experience at sea, fishermen, and others associated with maritime trade and industry such as riggers, shipwrights, and sailmakers. These men were essential to the economic well-being of the empire and were not to be conscripted by press gangs. However, simply identifying oneself as a member of a protected segment of British society was not enough to guarantee one's freedom. Each "protected man" was required to carry with him a document called a protection that identified him and his trade. If he could not produce his protection on demand by the press gang, he could be pressed without further question. Press gangs operated on land and sea. Impress cutters patrolled harbors and coastal areas searching for ships returning from voyages with men who might be pressed into service. Any officer of the Royal Navy could, when in need of men, stop English vessels on the high seas and press crewmen into service. Legally, foreigners were protected from the press, but this legality was often ignored, and the practice of pressing men at sea became common. In the eyes of the Royal Navy, all Englishmen were available for service even if they were on the ship of a foreign nation. Therefore, it was not uncommon for British naval vessels to stop American ships searching for English crewmen. During these searches, American sailors who could not prove their citizenship were often pressed. During the latter part of the eighteenth century, as England slugged its way through prolonged wars with France, the need for able seamen grew dramatically. During the peacetime that preceded the Napoleonic Wars, the Royal Navy had about 10,000 men; by the War of 1812, the number had risen to 140,000. The overwhelming majority of these men came from the press. To maintain the navy's strength, the press gangs were constantly at work. Not only did they have to replace men who were killed or died in service, but they also had to replace the countless vacancies created by desertion. Lord Nelson estimated that between 1793 and 1801 perhaps as many as 40,000 men deserted the navy. With demand for sailors always high and supply sometimes lacking, it is not surprising that the press gangs preyed from time to time on protected men, including Americans.[2]

Tensions with the British were once again at fever pitch and soon John Jay, Esq. (a signer of the treaty of 1783), was back in London again with another treaty intended to improve relations between the United States and England, this time with a document known as Jay's Treaty. This 1794 treaty was crafted by the dastardly Alexander Hamilton, well known to be an agent for the English banks and friend to the Rothschild family. Three years prior Alexander Hamilton had successfully set up his Rothschild-backed central banking system for the crown in downtown Philadelphia. Opened in 1791, America's first "central bank"* was called the First Bank of the United States and had a guaranteed twenty-year charter, which had been signed by George Washington.

The Jay Treaty of 1794 was passed by the Senate in the middle of the night and then rushed over the Atlantic where it was signed. This angered Thomas Jefferson and caused a stir between him and President Washington. Jefferson could not understand why Washington continued to deal with Hamilton. In return Washington could only comment that because of the war debt his hands were tied. According to

---

*A "central bank" handles the currency of a nation. It also controls interest rates and the money supply and can print and issue and loan the government money at interest. This practice forces the government to get money from the people to pay back these loans, and the resulting effect on both the people and the government is never-ending debt.

JOHN JAY BURNED IN EFFIGY.

Fig. 1.3. *Protest against the Jay Treaty of 1785.* Everett,
Fineartamerica.com

the Jay Treaty, America agreed to pay the king six hundred thousand
pounds sterling for losses incurred during the war. Imagine the outrage
Americans would feel if they found out about this. To make sure they
didn't, the Senate ordered the details of the treaty to be kept private.
However, they were outsmarted by Ben Franklin's grandson who snuck
a copy to the printing press and published it anyway. Congress was out-
raged by the publication and began working on the Alien and Sedition
Acts (1798), which allowed federal judges to prosecute editors and
publishers who reported the truth about the government, as Franklin's
grandson had done.

Americans were shocked by the Jay Treaty, which basically was a list
of demands they were ceding to the British, who were still dictating terms
more than a decade after they had supposedly lost the war. The Jay Treaty
didn't do much to improve shipping concerns; compensation relations
with the British, impressment, and naval harassment continued. But the
king had America in a corner, where he wanted her.

Fig. 1.4. *Bank of the United States on Third Street in Philadelphia* by William Birch (1800). Rare Book and Special Collections Division, Library of Congress

As a result of these events, by the summer of 1811 America was pretty much bankrupt. American sailors were continually harassed and impressed by the British Navy who, worried about American ships providing supplies to France, charged illegal porting taxes. These factors plus crippling trade restrictions allowed for a bitter mood toward England on the streets and within the halls of the White House.

The mood in England, at least in the halls of the king, was mutual. On January 24, 1811, Congress voted by the slimmest of margins not to renew the charter of the First Bank of the United States. This decision was primarily motivated by the fact that European bankers (the Rothschilds) owned 80 percent of the bank. After Congress refused to renew the charter, European investors withdrew more than seven million dollars from the bank, which led to a recession and ultimately to war.

Fig. 1.5. *Portrait of Nathan Mayer Rothschild* by Louis Amié Grosclaude (1830).
Isaac Newton Institute for Mathematical Sciences

Thomas Jefferson and Andrew Jackson had clamorously opposed this central bank, believing instead that the American people by way of Congress, not private or foreign interests, should command the money supply. Jackson and Jefferson were especially worried about the greatest of all bankers, the inheritor of the Rothschild family fortune: Nathan Rothschild.

The failure to renew the banking charter threw a monkey wrench into the financial monopoly that Nathan Rothschild was establishing in America and supposedly angered him so much that he allegedly warned to either renew the charter or face the disastrous consequences. And by consequences he meant staging another war against Britain in an effort to bring America back to colonial status. Rothschild then used one of his agents in America, Moses Taylor, to help him set up the National City Bank of New York in the summer of 1812. This was his way of maintaining a presence in America despite the recent defeat in Philadelphia. This National City Bank of New York survives today as Citibank.

Whether or not Nathan Rothschild actually said the words above or instructed the king to attack America has been impossible to prove thus far.[3] What we *can* prove is that less than five months after the First Bank of the United States closed its doors forever, the War of 1812 was on. However, it wasn't started by the British; it was started by the United States and declared by Congress on June 18, 1812. To most of the nation and to the war hawks in government it was viewed as a continuation of the Revolutionary War. It's even the war from which "The Star-Spangled Banner" comes.

The main reasons cited to start the War of 1812 were the continued impressment of American sailors and the British naval blockade of American goods intended for France. This new war also gave America a chance to completely take over British-owned lands in neighboring Canada. This was a move intended to expand our borders. The timing for the war was perfect, because Napoleon and his massive army were successfully on the offensive in Europe and most British resources and armed forces were preoccupied in engagement with him there.

The first six months of the War of 1812 were a stalemate, however, and the first-ever American-led invasion into Canada that November was a disaster. But after Napoleon's defeat in Russia his army was in retreat, and Britain was feeling much better about sending a larger fleet to deal with pesky America. William Ward, a British philanthropist and first Earl of Dudley, said in July of 1813, "I am glad of it with all my heart. When they declared war they thought it was pretty near over with us, and that their weight cast into the scale would decide our ruin. Luckily they were mistaken, and are likely to pay dear for their error."[4]

Dudley's prediction came true, but before the physical slaughter came the economic beheading, just as Nathan Rothschild had planned it.

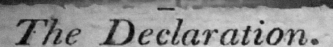

The Declaration.

AN ACT

Declaring War between the United Kingdom of Great Britain and Ireland and the dependencies thereof, and the United States of America and their Territories.

BE it enacted by the Senate and House of Representatives of the United States of America in Congress assembled, That WAR be and the same is hereby declared to exist between the

Fig. 1.6. A photograph of the Declaration of War (June 1812). PBS

By the fall of 1814, America's oceanic trade had dropped from $40 million in 1811 to $2.6 million in 1814, and revenues attributing to 90 percent of federal income fell by 80 percent, leaving the government virtually bankrupt. The Bureau of Public Debt reported that public debt more than doubled from $45.2 million in 1812 to $119.2 million by the time the war ended in 1815. America was also in dire straits financially as a result of invading Canada. With the tide of the Napoleonic Wars now turning in favor of the crown, for America to borrow money from a destitute France would be impossible.

The British captured Paris, and Napoleon abdicated his throne in April of 1814. He was sent to Elba Island for a short exile. England hoped the news of Napoleon's defeat would take the heart out of the American fighting spirit, and if it didn't, the unequaled havoc it would soon begin to wreak on the country should.

America lost the bloodiest battle of the war (Lundy's Lane) on July 25, 1814, when seventeen hundred soldiers, along with the dream of annexing Canada, died a few miles west of Niagara Falls. A month later the British raped and pillaged their way through Delaware, Pennsylvania,

Fig. 1.7. *Capture and Burning of Washington by the British*
(1876 wood engraving)

and Maryland, ending up at the White House, where they promptly burned the iconic building and several other government buildings to the ground. The included fire damage to the Senate and House wings, a destabilized colonnade in the House of Representatives shored up with firewood to prevent its collapse, and only a shell of the rotunda remaining.

The British had successfully torched the Capitol, the Library of Congress, and almost all records pertaining to the first thirty-eight years of America's government. If it weren't for a freak hurricane and a series of even freakier tornados that appeared out of nowhere to halt any further British destruction, who knows just how bad things could have gotten for the newly formed nation?[5]

By destroying government records, the British were able to lay waste to the Constitution's newly adopted Thirteenth Amendment. This amendment prevented anyone who held a title of nobility or honor from serving in the government, much like the esquire status that some

Fig. 1.8. *Capture of the City of Washington*
by Paul de Rapin-Thoyras (1814)

Fig. 1.9. The ruins of the U.S. Capitol following British attempts
to burn the building by George Munger (1814)

of our founding fathers enjoyed. The Thirteenth Amendment basically made it illegal for lawyers to serve in the government! All lawyers of the time had to be granted a license by the International Bar Association, which of course was chartered by the king of England and headquartered in London. Thought to have been destroyed during the war, the original records of the Thirteenth Amendment have since been found in the archives of the British Museum in London and in various state archives, including the public library at Belfast, Maine, where archivists accidently discovered its proclamations in a rare Constitution printed in 1825.[6] This forgotten amendment was successfully added to the Constitution in 1819, but despite what seemed like a huge victory against tyranny, it slowly faded into obscurity and was wiped clean from memory almost altogether. In fact, during the Civil War it was replaced with a brand-new Thirteenth Amendment despite never having been lawfully repealed.

The war ended on a somewhat positive note for America, as a new national hero emerged in General Andrew Jackson after his miraculous victory during the Battle of New Orleans. Jackson was on his way to prominence and the presidency, which meant an eventual head-on collision with the Rothschilds. As for the British, the war ended in a truce with the signing of the Treaty of Ghent in 1814, which was fine by them considering that their real victory was the final defeat of Napoleon at Waterloo. Basically nothing on the surface changed at all between us and them, and America was spared any more British-led invasions until the arrival of the Beatles in 1961. As usual, the only real losers of the War of 1812 were the Native Americans who lost a lot more of their land as a result. The famed Shawnee tribal chief Tecumseh famously said, "You want, by your distinctions of Indian tribes, in allotting to each a particular tract of land, to make them to war with each other. You never see an Indian come and endeavor to make the white people do so."[7]

In 1812, Tecumseh aligned with the British and sacked Fort Detroit before dying at the Battle of the Thames in Ontario the next year. The remainder of his army surrendered, and the Native Americans contin-

Fig. 1.10. *The Battle of New Orleans* by Jean Hyacinthe de Laclotte (1815).
New Orleans Museum of Art

ued to be pushed out of their ancestral homelands. For America the War of 1812 became the war in which it had finally gained its independence and become an important and permanent fixture on the world stage. However, it was also a victory for the crown and the Rothschilds' banking schemes. Because of its massive war debt and its bankrupted economy, America was once again planning on chartering a central bank. As 1816 loomed, Nathan Rothschild waited in the wings, drooling at the prospects.

2
The Rothschilds Win Again

1815–1825

Scarlet Begonias

As I picked up my matches and was closing the door,
I had one of those flashes I'd been there before, been
*   there before.*
Well, I ain't always right but I've never been wrong.
Seldom turns out the way it does in a song.
Once in a while you get shown the light
In the strangest of places if you look at it right.

GRATEFUL DEAD

America preaches integration and practices segregation.

MALCOLM X

As the War of 1812 and the Napoleonic Wars were ending the
Rothschild dynasty was entering its prime. From 1813 to 1815, five
Rothschild brothers would largely finance the British war efforts
against Napoleon while also supplying gold to the same army it was
fighting against. Nathan Rothschild happened to be in England supplying money to the Duke of Wellington's armies while Jacob Rothschild

was in France supplying money to Napoleon's army, thus cleverly funding both sides of the war.

The Rothschild bankers loved wars, because by playing both sides they were guaranteed by the government to be recipients of massive amounts of money via hyperinflation from the debt they helped create. They didn't care who won; they just wanted to have a war! The Rothschilds owed their dynasty to wars and more specifically to Napoleon's epic defeat at Waterloo. Because they owned a series of banks spread throughout Europe, the family had unparalleled access to new information. Centuries before the existence of Twitter, the Rothschilds used a network of secret couriers who traveled on clandestine routes, gaining and passing on knowledge that would keep the Rothschild bankers always one step ahead of the curve.

These Rothschild couriers were in fact the only nonmilitary personnel allowed access through English and French blockades. With intelligence gained from these secret couriers Nathan Rothschild could control the buying and selling on the British Stock Exchange. Rothworth, one of Nathan's trustworthy couriers, was able to deliver the outcome of the Battle of Waterloo twenty-four hours earlier than Lord Wellington's courier. This made it possible for the Rothschilds to sell all of their British bonds and start rumors on the floor that the British had lost the war. This made all of the other traders sell their bonds in Britain as well, as panic swept the London streets. The value of the bonds then plummeted to almost nothing, allowing the Rothschilds to begin secretly buying back the bonds for a matter of mere pennies. When news finally broke that the British had won the war the bonds almost doubled in price, becoming as high as they had been the day before Nathan Rothschild earned a return of twenty to one on his investment.

This legendary economic act helped to establish the Bank of England and gave the Rothschild family complete control of the British economy—an economy soon to be the financial center of the world after Napoleon's defeat at Waterloo in 1815. This legendary conspiracy tale, which is almost hard to believe, actually happened even though history was slow to reveal it. The *Argus,* a newspaper in Melbourne, Australia, leaked the story in 1918 in a small paragraph nestled between advertisements and local military stories.

Top of Form, Bottom of Form
The True Waterloo Story

In Sir Henry Lucy's "Diary of a Journalist" in the London *Sunday Times,* appears the following story of the Rothschilds and Waterloo—Divers versions are enshrined in history of the circumstances under which old Nathan Meyer Rothschild, founder of the family, obtained the earliest exclusive information of the Battle of Waterloo. One of the favourite stories is that he accompanied Wellington's forces disguised as a sutler (civilian merchant), and as soon as the fortunes of the day were decided, posted off to London, where he made the best of the markets. One of his grandsons, a partner in the London house, tells me the true story, which, he adds, has never been published. His grandfather, who settled in London whilst his elder brother, Anselme, remained at Frankfort, and his second brother, Salomon, opened a branch of the bank at Vienna, established relations with the English Government, acting as their agent in buying gold, much needed to carry on the campaign against Napoleon. For the purposes of his business, Nathan Meyer had in his pay a swift sailing lugger, which kept him in correspondence with his brothers and other friends on the Continent. One day in June, 1815, the captain of the lugger, fresh from a trip across the Channel, came upon Rothschild. He had, in quite a casual way, put in his pocket a Dutch newspaper. Looking it over, Rothschild found an account of the Battle of Waterloo, brief, but so unfaltering and evidently authentic that he straightway went on Change and bought Consols by the bucketful. They were on this particular day beaten down lower than ever, the last news from the seat of war not coming down later than an account of the affair at Quatre Bras, represented as a check to Wellington. When, later, the Government received official dispatches describing Bonaparte's rout, the Funds went up by leaps and bounds, and the fortunes of the house of Rothschild were established on a princely scale.[1]

Before his epic defeat at Waterloo, Napoleon said, "When a government is dependent upon bankers for money, they and not the leaders of the government control the situation, since the hand that gives is above the hand that takes. . . . Money has no motherland; financiers are without patriotism and without decency; their sole object is gain."[2] Napoleon had it right, but the Battle of Waterloo would be his final fight as he mysteriously died in exile six years later.

Nathan's insider trading stratagem would help secure the Rothschild empire for centuries to come; the family practically invented modern finance. A hundred years after Napoleon's defeat, grandchildren of Nathan Rothschild were in court asking a judge to suppress the insider trading information that was about to go public in a new biography of the family. But the court denied their request, allowed the book to be published, and ordered them to pay the court costs. This was a rare victory against the Rothschilds, but in 1816 all they did was win, because

Fig. 2.1. *Battle of Waterloo* by William Sadler (1815)

America was in financial ruin and in need of another central bank to help pay off its debts.

The extremely expensive War of 1812 basically forced America to recharter another Rothschild-dominated central bank. Naturally this new bank would be named the Second Bank of the United States, and, despite much opposition and President Madison's four attempts to veto it, the bank was given the green light in 1816 with a new twenty-year charter. The first act of the newly established Second Bank would be a *loan* of $60 million to the government. The Second Bank was designed by Master Mason and architect William Strickland and finally opened in 1818. It issued as many banknotes as it wanted, given that it was exempt from state taxes. It would soon begin to issue more notes than it could possibly be able to pay for. Inflation and the money supply were high throughout the country thanks to a steady stream of banks that had opened in western places like Kentucky and Tennessee. These and all other banks relied on the currency issued from the central bank back in Philadelphia.

By the summer of 1819 the money flow, mostly from loans, had been issued so freely throughout America that times were looking better than they had in a long while. The good times were soon over, however, as the central bank put a squeeze on the money supply, causing an instant depression. This inflation and deflation of the currency left a good chunk of western landowners unable to pay their debts, which allowed the banks to begin purchasing large tracts of western lands for less than half their value. The Rothschild-designed boom-and-bust cycle was on; panic was in the streets, and those that weren't part of the club would soon find themselves close to financial ruin. G. Edward Griffin described this banking scheme in 1994.

> It is widely believed that panics, boom-and-bust cycles, and depressions are caused by unbridled competition between banks; thus the need for government regulation. The truth is just the opposite. These disruptions in the free market are the result of government

prevention of competition by the granting of monopolistic power to the central bank.³

The Panic of 1819 is often described as America's first major financial crisis. It was, in fact, part of a *worldwide* financial panic, given that the Rothschilds were also wrecking the economies of France and Prussia. America's crisis was marked by widespread unemployment as well as bank failures and foreclosures. Even the Second Bank was in crisis; Congress was threatening to shut it down due to the public's massive disapproval of the sudden financial depression, which, they figured, was caused by the newly established bank. A reorganizing regime change came to the Second Bank as its former head, William Jones, resigned and Langdon Cheves took over as its new president.

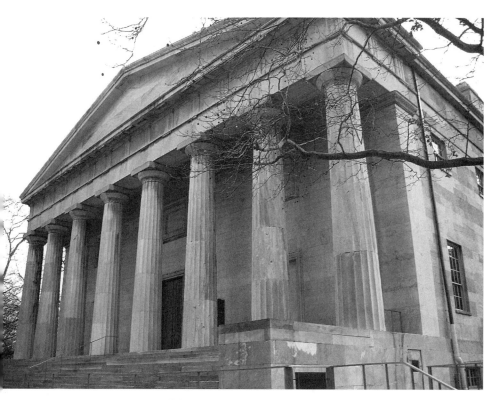

Figs. 2.2. A view of the Second Bank of the United States (2013).
Photo by Xaviant Haze

Fig. 2.3. The Panic of 1819, "The Panic in Wall Street," *Harper's Weekly*, October 10, 1857. Courtesy of the Woodruff Library, Emory University, Atlanta, Georgia

Cheves was a former Speaker of the House and longtime Rothschild supporter. He even brought to the bank with him the Rothschild financial protégée, Nicholas Biddle. Biddle was one of the villains discussed in the first book of this series:* the shady editor of Meriwether Lewis's journal and known Rothschild agent. Biddle joined the Second Bank's board of directors just in time for a bird's-eye view of the Panic of 1819. Biddle became the bank's president in 1822.

The economic depression continued throughout Biddle's tenure, but the Rothschilds' central banking dream of controlling the American economy was working to perfection. As is explained further by *Conspiracy Theories in American History: An Encyclopedia:*

As director of the Second Bank of the United States, and proponent of a centralized financial system for the United States, Nicholas

---

The Suppressed History of America: The Murder of Meriwether Lewis and the Mysterious Discoveries of the Lewis and Clark Expeditions, by Paul Schrag and Xaviant Haze (Rochester, Vt.: Bear & Company, 2011).

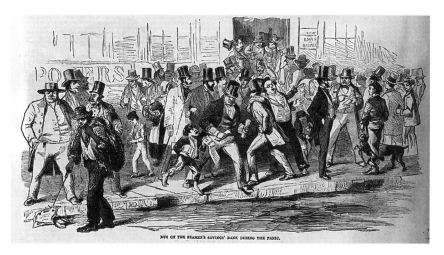

Fig. 2.4. The Panic of 1819, "Run on the Seamen's Bank."
Harper's Weekly, October 31, 1857

Biddle (1786–1844) was the target of accusations that he led a conspiracy of wealthy aristocrats to control the national economy. Biddle, born in Philadelphia in 1786, was everything that President Andrew Jackson considered dangerous—a graduate of Princeton, editor of a literary journal and of several volumes of the journals of the Lewis and Clark expedition, and, as a young man, a secretary to the U.S diplomatic mission to tsarist Russia. All of Biddle's experiences, especially exposure to the economic chaos of early-nineteenth-century Russia, and the vast infrastructure demanded by the opening of the American West, led him to believe that the United States needed the strength of a central bank. Biddle, who had been on the board of directors since 1819, took control of the bank in 1823. From its chartering in 1816, the Second Bank was mired in controversy, sparking the Supreme Court case *McCulloch v. Maryland,* in which Congress was shown to have the legal power to charter the institution. The economic panic of 1819, while not caused by the establishment of the bank, was largely blamed on the bank by unhappy small farmers, westerners, and supporters of state banks. Biddle believed that the bank's director should be apolitical, but when opposition to his institution surged he sought allies in Congress, including Daniel Webster and Henry Clay. Biddle and his supporters agreed that the nation needed ready access to funds capable of supporting large-scale military actions, like that waged in the War of 1812, and favored strict regulation of state banks.[4]

The Panic of 1819 lasted until 1824. Within this period mortgage and agricultural prices were slashed in half, and investments into western lands almost disappeared. Debtors' prisons still existed, and in Philadelphia alone more than eighteen hundred people were sent there. Nearly 30 percent of the country was unemployed, and for the first time in American history urban poverty and homelessness became public talking points. Protests were staged in major cities, and the people affected by the crisis proposed new laws to provide debt relief as well as champion the permanent abolition of debtors' prisons. (Many Americans would be shocked to discover that debtors' prisons have returned today and are filled with people from across the country who have been jailed for not paying their fines.[5])

By 1824 the panic was over, but manufacturing interests were still a mess given that high tariffs and competition from foreign imports reduced the flow of international trade. The panic left a lasting impression on American politics: public outcry led to reformed state constitutions and tighter restrictions on voting as well as a heightened awareness of banking and corporate monopolies. The panic also irritated war hero Andrew Jackson, who was now the senator of Tennessee and setting his sights on running for president, with the intention of shutting down the central bank once and for all.

While the Rothschild central banking scheme was starting to take over the world, it was still just getting established in post-revolutionary America. This new country that the Rothschilds would seek to control was a historical and cultural anomaly in many ways. Not only were its Native people trying to avoid genocide, but America had a secret history of once being populated by ancient giants. When the young nation began to slowly crawl its way out of the depression caused by the Panic

Fig. 2.5. Nicholas Biddle engraved by John Sartain (1831).
Source of image, Nicholas B. Wainwright, Quakerquilts

of 1819, astonishing discoveries of the bones of ancient giants were revealed as new lands were settled.

In 1820 an ancient graveyard was discovered in Erie, Pennsylvania, on land owned and excavated by two doctors. When they began digging up some of the bodies in the graveyard they were shocked at the immense size of some of the skeletons. The following excerpt is from the *History of Erie County, Volume 1.*

When the roadway of the Philadelphia & Erie Railroad, where it passes through the Warfel farm, was being widened, another deposit of bones was dug up and summarily deposed of as before (thrown in a neighboring ditch). Among the skeletons was one of a giant, side by side with a smaller one, probably that of his wife. The arm and leg bones of this Native American Goliath were about one-half longer than those of the tallest man among the laborers; the skull was immensely large; the lower jawbone easily slipped over the face and whiskers of a full-faced man, and the teeth were in a perfect state of preservation. Another skeleton was dug up in Conneaut Township a few years ago which was quite as remarkable in its dimensions. As in the other instance, a comparison was made with the largest man in the neighborhood, and the jawbone readily covered his face, while the lower bone of the leg was nearly a foot longer than the one with which it was measured, indicating that the man must have been eight to ten feet in height. The bones of a flathead were turned up in the same township some two years ago with a skull of unusual size. Relics of a former time have been gathered in that section by the pail full, and among other curiosities a brass watch was found that was as big as a common saucer.[6]

Not only were ancient giant skulls and bones discovered but also giant brass watches! In 1821 giant bones were discovered in Williamson County, Tennessee, near what appeared to be an ancient stone fortification. In his book *The Natural and Aboriginal History of Tennessee* author John Haywood describes various discoveries of ancient giants and dwarfish pigmies whose existence appeared to predate the local Native tribes. Tennessee has a rich history of giant skeletons being discovered in graves and mound sites, all of which Haywood wrote about. He was a lawyer and an intellectual who, in addition to writing several law books, was eventually appointed to the Tennessee Supreme Court of Errors and Appeals. His belief that the aboriginal peoples of Tennessee descended from the ancient Hebrews caused a bit of controversy in his day. He also claimed that these aborigines were killed off by the ancient giants who inhabited most of the Midwest. Haywood writes:

First, then—of their Size, This is ascertained by the length and dimensions of the skeletons which are found in East and West Tennessee. These will prove demonstratively, that the ancient inhabitants of this country, either the primitive or secondary settlers, were of gigantic stature, compared with the present races. . . . On the farm of Mr. John Miller, of White county, are a number of small graves, and also many large ones, the bones in which show that the bodies to which they belonged, when alive, must have been seven feet high and upward. About the year 1814, Mr. Lawrence found, in Scarborough's cave . . . about 12 or 15 miles from Sparta, in a little room in the cave, many human bones of a monstrous size. He took a jaw bone and applied it to his own face, and when his chin touched the concave of the chin bone, the hinder ends of the jaw bone did not touch the skin of his face on either side. He took a thigh bone, and applied the upper end of it to his own hip joint, and the lower end reached four inches below the knee joint. Mr. Andrew Bryan saw a grave opened about 4 miles northwardly from Sparta . . . he took a thigh bone, and raising up his knee, he applied the knee joint of the bone to the extreme length of his own knee and the upper end of the bone passed out behind him as far as the full width of his body. Mr. Lawrence is about 5 feet, 10 inches high, and Mr. Bryan about 5 feet, 9. Mr. Sharp Whitley was in a cave near the place, where Mr. Bryan saw the graves opened. In it were many of these bones. The skulls lie plentifully in it, and all the other bones of the human body all in proportion, and of monstrous size. Human bones were taken out of a mound on the Tennessee river, below Kingston, which Mr. Brown saw measured, by Mr. Simms the thigh bones of those skeletons, when applied to Mr. Simms's thigh, were an inch and a half longer than his, from the point of his hip to his knee: supposing the whole frame to have been in the same proportion the body it belonged to must have been seven feet high or upward. Many bones in the mounds there are of equal size. . . . Col. William Sheppard, late of North Carolina, in the year 1807, dug up, on the plantation of Col. Joel Lewis, 2 miles from Nashville, the jaw bones of a man, which easily covered the whole chin and jaw of Col. Lewis, a man of large size. Some years afterward, Mr. Cassady dug up a skeleton from under a small mound near the large one at Bledsoe's lick, in Sumner county, which measured little short of seven feet in length. Human bones have been dug up at the plantation where Judge Overton now lives, four miles southwestwardly from Nashville. These bones were of extraordinary size. The under jaw bone of one skeleton very easily slipped over the jaw of Mr. Childress, a stout man, full fleshed, very robust, and considerably over the common size. . . . About ten miles from Sparta, in White county, a conical mound was lately opened, and in the center of it was a skeleton eight feet in length. . . . With this skeleton was found another nearly of the same size, with the top of his head flat, and his eyes placed apparently in the upper part of his forehead.[7]

In 1822 another giant skeleton was found in Pennsylvania. It measured eight feet two inches in length and was discovered by a man known as General Mckean who, while digging a cellar, struck a rock surface that rang hollow. Intrigued, he broke through the cover stone to discover two tombs, each nine feet deep. Inside one of the tombs was a giant eight-foot skeleton whose ancient bones were soft and crumbled easily after successfully being measured. As a testament to the old age of these tombs, a three-foot-thick pine tree was found growing out of them.

Less than two hundred miles away in 1822 in East Haven, Connecticut, a Native American burial ground produced more giant discoveries. John Warner Barber of the Connecticut Historical Collections writes in *History and Antiquities of Every Connecticut Town:*

Fig. 2.6. Two giant skulls found in Wisconsin.
Moundbuilder.blogspot.com

The great burying place of the Indian tribes in this town and vicinity, is on the North end of the hill on which the fort stands, which, anciently, in allusion to this place, was called Grave Hill. Some of the graves have been leveled by the plow, but many of them are yet visible. In the year 1822, I examined three of these graves. At the depth of about three feet and a half the sandstone appears, on which the bodies are laid, without any appearance of a wrapper or enclosure. They all lay in the direction of southwest and northeast—the head toward the west. Of two of them, the arms lay by the side; the other had the arms across the body, after the manner of the white people. The large bones and teeth were in a sound state. The thighbones of one measured 19 inches in length, the leg bone 18, and the arm from the elbow to the shoulder 13. By measuring the skeleton as it lay, it was concluded to be of a man six and a half feet high.[8]

Fig. 2.7. Giant skeleton found in an Ohio mound.
Moundbuilder.blogspot.com

In 1824 a plethora of mysterious American giants were being dug out of the mounds that littered the Ohio Valley region. Also that year another American giant was heading to the presidency. Tennessee senator Andrew Jackson's candidacy began at the grassroots level, but once word spread that the hero of New Orleans was running for president he quickly emerged as a popular favorite. This sudden political threat emerged out of nowhere, leaving Rothschild sympathizers like House Speaker Henry Clay, presidential front-runner John Quincy Adams, and secretary of war and future vice president John C. Calhoun extremely worried about the upcoming election.

Fig. 2.8. An Ohio mound by the highway. Moundbuilder.blogspot.com

Jackson's march toward the White House in 1824 was a key political event in American history and an early black eye in the fight against
the central banking powers. Jackson was by far the most popular candidate on the campaign trail and easily finished first in the popular voting. Based on this alone Jackson should have been president, but the fix
was in, and Jackson knew it when the ticker tape parade didn't begin.
Despite winning the Electoral College vote, Jackson fell short of the
required majority, thus leaving the final word in the hands of the House
of Representatives. But instead of ratifying the people's choice they
decided to make John Quincy Adams president instead. The people
were furious at this, and threats of protests and riots were widespread.

The defeat of Jackson was a temporary Rothschild victory, added
to their victory a year earlier when they had gained control over the
Vatican's finances after the pope had begged Nathan Rothschild for a
loan. For Jackson the unique experience made him the first candidate
to ever win the popular vote by a landslide yet still lose the presidency
by not winning the Electoral College vote.

Theories about a conspiracy to keep Jackson out of the White House spread across America a week after the dirty deed had been done. Jackson was furious and announced that the decision to make Adams president was a "corrupt bargain" against the people and him. Jackson was known for his fiery temper; he was after all a grizzly war veteran who had survived gun battles, with bullets still lodged in his body. He had also killed men in duels and was imagining dueling Nicholas Biddle when he penned his vehement response to losing the presidency: "So you see, the Judas of the West has closed the contract and will receive the thirty pieces of silver. His end will be the same. Was there ever witnessed such a bare-faced corruption in any country before?"[9]

Jackson supporters tried to undermine the new administration's every move, while Missouri senator Thomas Hart Benton (not to be confused with the painter of the same name) led a congressional investigation of corruption. Whether a corrupt bargain or not, the Adams presidency was being guided by the actions of the Second Bank and its newly appointed director, Nicholas Biddle. Biddle was about to revolutionize the way corporations did business in the modern world, thereby setting an example that most prominent businesses would follow in the century to come.

With his power at the bank, Biddle worked to maximize his influence by forging ties and extending loans to politicians, lawmakers, congressmen, military leaders, and a few political journalists who chose to write with only the good side of their pen. Biddle even employed prominent congressional leaders like Henry Clay and Daniel Webster as private capacity lawyers. These men, of course, were friends with the new president and members of his cabinet. All of them opposed Andrew Jackson and his ideas about central banking, a practice that Jackson referred to as the "Hydra of corruption."

But Jackson was ahead of the pack when it came to understanding the dangerous central banking scheme in the 1820s. To most people of the time as well, banks were seen as suspect institutions that loaned paper money and encouraged reckless investments and loans, all with-

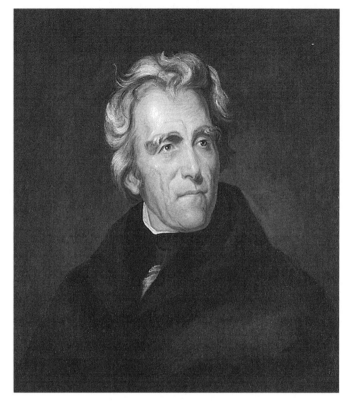

Fig. 2.10. Andrew Jackson portrait attributed to Thomas Sully (1824)

out the familiar weight of silver and gold to back them. These feelings weren't restored after the Panic of 1819. Instead, the people were even more soured after Jackson had lost the presidency.

A few months before the election had been decided Jackson and Biddle had dinner together. Jackson bit his tongue so as to not say anything he would later regret. Nonetheless, the meeting confirmed to Biddle that Jackson was not going to remain silent on the issue of the central bank. Indeed, Jackson proceeded to school Biddle on the history of central banking, claiming that he had been "afraid" of banks ever since learning about the South Sea Bubble market fiasco, a scheme that had crashed the British stock market in 1711. He then elaborated on the boom-and-bust cycles that banks like Biddle's were responsible for, including the most recent events relating to the War of 1812 and the Panic of 1819. Jackson made it clear to Biddle that he was no fan of central banking or the Rothschilds. After that dinner with Jackson, Biddle knew what had to be done, and, with his influence and money, he saw to it that Jackson was denied the presidency, popular opinion be damned.

Andrew Jackson had barely escaped financial ruin during the Panic of 1819 and knew that most Americans hadn't been so lucky. This harrowing experience made the fight against the central bank personal for Jackson, and, as 1824 ended, he withdrew from office and began to focus solely on the next upcoming presidential election. As stated earlier, his initial loss of the White House had fueled rumors of government conspiracies and shady deals being made within the halls of Congress. The people had spoken, and Jackson was listening, lacing up his gloves and ready to step into the ring again, but this time with a whole new political party at his disposal.

3
Andrew Jackson Steps into the Arena

1826–1831

AmeriKKKan History X

*When I think of ameriKKKa I think of greed, laissez-faire
 capitalism, and 1% wealth.*

*School never taught me about the first Europeans to find
 ameriKKKa who happened to be Welsh. The first
 Europeans integrated, not desicrated. Red-haired people
 who viewed the Natives as equal—No Bibles, rifles,
 smallpox, or disease.*

*Did you know in the Grand Canyon they found ancient-
 coins belonging to the Chinese?*

This was way before Columbus got lost on the 7 seas.

*Did your teacher tell you about the time when—The first
 visitors were Mayan?*

Or when the First People called this land Turtle Island?

Or did ya learn that from KRS rhyming?

*Egyptians, Khemtians, all here before the Pilgrims and
 demons.*

AmeriKKKan demoKKKracy, apple pies, hypocrisy, racism,

and ameriKKKan lies—Most Black Citizens couldn't
even vote until the Voting Rights Act of 1965.
AmeriKKKa wasn't founded on democracy, open yo' eyes.
Slavery, whips, land-grabs aplenty
Women couldn't even vote until 1920.
See I bring it back a ton, to the First Sun, to the First One,
to your first drink of colostrum. Back to the block, before
bee-bop, before Plymouth Rock
All the way back to the time of Enoch.

JOSH RIZEBERG

History is a set of lies that people have agreed upon.

NAPOLEON

In 1825 most of the American public still wanted Andrew Jackson to be president. They also wanted the corrupt congressmen who had voted against him kicked out of office for good. As the congressional elections of 1826 got under way, many were surprised that a new political organization fronted by Jackson began to emerge. The Democratic Party was born in the summer of 1826 by Jackson and a handful of like-minded men who wanted to expand on the philosophies of Thomas Jefferson and put an end to the current, elite-driven rule of those in the government.

The congressional campaign was off to a quick start as Jackson took aim at one of his biggest opponents, the Speaker of the House and central bank advocate Henry Clay. In Clay's home state of Kentucky, Jackson threw a huge barbecue for the members of Congress who had voted for him and announced that he was leaving his seat in the Senate to once again run for president. Jackson wanted Congress to know that the president should be elected by the people, not by the bargaining powers of those in the nation's capital. The warning was clear as a new wave of Jackson supporters were elected to Congress and soon began to oppose most of President Adams's financial and governmental projects.

The congressional elections of 1826 saw many Adams and Clay supporters lose their seats in Congress. Others, seeing which way the wind was now blowing, jumped ship to join the Jackson bandwagon. With less than two years left in power, the Adams-Clay faction evolved into the Whig Party and began to hurl as much dirt as they could at Jackson in the press. But Jackson would soon have a press of his own to counter the attacks as a group of wealthy and influential men from Washington, D.C., and New York aligned to have his back.

The wealthy Manhattan senator Martin Van Buren was on board with Jackson, as well as John Henry Eaton and Duff Green, two Southerners who bought out and took over the *United States Telegraph*. Popularly known as the *Telegraph,* it would serve as Jackson's main promoter, championing him to the public by way of its content and its advertising. With a national newspaper to fight back against the Rothschilds' domination of the press, Jackson was ready to take the fight center stage as the 1828 presidential election got under way. It would be the rematch the people had been waiting for as the two opponents, who had previously squared off in what had been known as the "corrupt bargain" four years earlier, were set to do political battle once more.

This time, however, Jackson not only had his usual support from the South, but he had also managed to add New York's most powerful political broker, Martin Van Buren, to the fold. With this support from the influential Van Buren, Jackson's political appeal to the working masses in the North tripled. The move by Van Buren to back Jackson caused a ripple of panic throughout Congress and made the already nervous Adams and Clay tremble in their boots. Furthermore, the move by Van Buren sent shock waves through the halls of the central bank in Philadelphia and caused a downsizing of employees at the Rothschild-dominated National Bank in New York.

With a return to the two-party system the 1828 election served as the precursor to the presidential elections we know today. The

Republicans were represented by sitting president Adams, against Jackson's newly formed Democratic loyalists who were organized by New York's political seer, Martin Van Buren. The significance of the 1828 election was that for the first time ever a champion of the common people and a non-elitist could be elected president. Because of this, and because of the concerns about America's banking system, the intense personal attacks between the president, John Quincy Adams, and the challenger, Andrew Jackson, became sordid front-page news.

But apart from the sharing of a long history of public service together, the two men could not have been more different. Adams, the son of founding father and second president, John Adams, was a career politician who had started his career as a diplomat while still a teenager. Viewed as a refined "Yankee" elitist, Adams was soon slandered by Jackson supporters as a pimp who provided underage girls to the Russian tsar, played billiards in the White House, and took outlandish vacations on the taxpayers' dime—allegations that were at least halfway true.

Adams retreated from the claims and never publicly commented on the accusations. (Neither did he write anything at all in his personal diaries until after the election.) By the time the votes were cast, both men's lives would be the subject of wild tabloid stories, replete with garish charges of murder and adultery. Most of the outlandish fodder, however, was reserved for Jackson, whose life of military exploits—coupled with a bad temper—lavished a goldmine of potential material upon newspapers everywhere.

Jackson was famous for his violent and controversial life. It had been an incredibly hard one, and even harder to imagine. He had enlisted in the Continental Army as a twelve-year-old boy and during the Revolutionary War ran important packages across the front lines. Jackson was eventually captured by the British, making him the only president to ever have been a prisoner of war. Forced to be a servant to a British major, Jackson was left with a scar on his face from a knife slash after he refused to spit shine the redcoat major's boots. His scar remained and so did his hatred. Jackson was eventually released as part

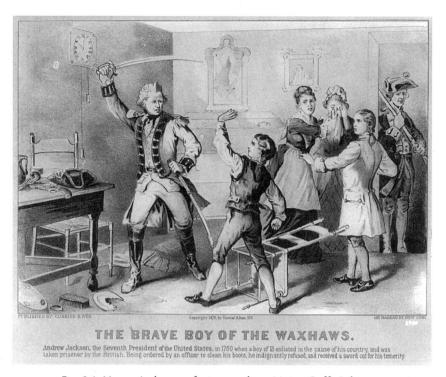

THE BRAVE BOY OF THE WAXHAWS.

Andrew Jackson, the Seventh President of the United States, in 1780 when a boy of 13 enlisted in the cause of his country, and was taken prisoner by the British. Being ordered by an officer to clean his boots, he indignantly refused, and received a sword cut for his temerity.

Fig. 3.1. Young Jackson refusing to clean Major Coffin's boots.
Lithograph (1876) by Currier & Ives

of a prisoner exchange program a year later, but the war and succeeding illnesses eventually killed Jackson's entire family, making him an orphan at fourteen.

Now alone, Jackson moved south to Tennessee, where he practiced frontier law, which at the time was basically one step removed from bare-knuckle boxing and wrestling in the swamp to decide the outcome of a legal quarrel. The same year that Tennessee became an official state Jackson wasted no time in becoming a congressman. He also served as the commander of the Tennessee militia and a colonel in the army reserves. His military career would soon be epic as he soundly defeated the notorious "Red Stick" tribe with the help of Sam Houston and Davy Crockett at the Battle of Horseshoe Bend in 1814 and somehow managed to miraculously destroy the British at the Battle of New Orleans in 1815.

Fig. 3.2. Andrew Jackson refusing to shake hands at
the Battle of Horseshoe Bend in 1814

With his ragtag army of sailors, militiamen, Choctaws, free blacks, and pirates, Jackson and his nearly four thousand troops and eight artillery cannons hunkered down, creating a fortified line in the swamps, hoping to slow the British invasion. Despite being outnumbered two to one, Jackson's army mangled the British forces and even killed all three of their senior commanding officers. Jackson's line held, and the British retreated back home with their tails between their legs. Incredibly, Jackson's army suffered only thirteen deaths, and less than a hundred men were wounded. Jackson fought the Native Americans as much as he fought the British, with victories over the Seminole and Creek tribes from Florida, which eventually served as the impetus for the Adams-Onis Treaty that resulted in the Spanish ceding Florida to the United States. His status as a war hero and Indian fighter, along with his notions about how to deal with corrupt politicians and bankers, made him the front-runner of the presidential election of 1828. This brought out the worst from the Rothschild-backed newspapers, which ridiculed Jackson as a dim-witted thug and murderer.

By the time of the election Jackson had participated in a mind-blowing number of duels; 103 to be exact. But duels in those days were not regarded as spectacles of outlaws as depicted in movies set in the Old West. They were more about principles and honor. The duelers did not take ten steps and then shoot. Instead, they would stand at a considerable distance from each other and fire their guns into the air, purposefully missing their opponent. On the rare occasion when the duelers were serious, people indeed were killed. However, most were just wounded, and the majority of duels ended up unresolved in terms of winner and loser. A number of Jackson's duels were settled without a shot ever having been fired.

When participating in a duel, Jackson was a menace to behold; he wore an oversized trench coat that hung off his lanky six-foot-two-inch frame, making him an imposing figure to behold.

Jackson's first documented duel was against fellow war hero and attorney Waightstill Avery in 1788. The two had faced off in a Tennessee civil suit where the more experienced Avery outclassed Jackson, turning one of Jackson's arguments against him so badly that an embarrassed and embittered Jackson felt he had been slighted. Jackson wasted no time in issuing a challenge to a duel, which he placed in an old law book that he craftily gave Avery. But Avery didn't take the challenge seriously until a day later when, back at court, Jackson kept pestering him for a showdown. The pair agreed upon a location and set the duel for the following night. By then, however, cooler heads had prevailed and despite both stepping onto the field of battle, neither wanted to hurt the other and thus both men fired shots into the air. They went on to shake hands and make up with a night of drinking and eventually became close friends.

Jackson's second documented duel was against Tennessee governor John Sevier in 1804.

The build-up to Andrew Jackson's duel with John Sevier, the first Governor of Tennessee, took a couple of years of bitter rivalry to develop into a duel. The build-up to this rivalry began after John Sevier served three consecutive terms as Governor of Tennessee before stepping down due to term limits. In his place Andrew Jackson's friend, Archibald Roane, was elected Governor. Sevier decided to run for the post of Commander of the Militia after his three-term limit was up. His opponent for the post was Jackson, and the election that followed was close enough to be determined a draw.

According to Tennessee law at the time it was then up to the Governor (Jackson's friend) to choose the next militia commander. Governor Roane chose Jackson. This defeat to Jackson left Sevier feeling bitter, especially since Sevier had a great deal more military experience than Jackson at this time. Since Governor terms lasted only two years in Tennessee and since there was no term limit to the number of times you could be Governor during your life, Sevier chose to run for Governor against Roane in the next election. During the election Roane, with Jackson backing him, accused Sevier of bribery and fraud because they believed that Sevier had changed the original land claims for the state of Tennessee. This hurt Sevier's reputation, but did not stop him from defeating Roane for the Governor's seat.

With Sevier now the Governor again, and Jackson still the Commander of the Militia, both men saw each other on a regular basis, and Sevier had not forgotten Jackson's accusations during the election. During a heated exchange out in the courthouse square in Knoxville, Sevier accused Jackson of adultery. This accusation led to shots being fired (no one was hurt), and Jackson having to be pulled away from Sevier. The next day he sent Sevier a letter challenging him to a duel. After some disagreements regarding where they were to duel (dueling in Tennessee was illegal) they settled on meeting at Southwest Point (in Virginia at the time) to settle their feud. Accounts differ as to what happened next, but Jackson arrived at the agreed location first, waiting several hours for Sevier, who had been delayed. After a while, Jackson, believing Sevier was not going to show up, began to head back to Knoxville when he encountered Sevier on the road heading to the agreed location. Both men began exchanging insults on the road, and during the argument Sevier's horse ran off with his firearms.

Jackson pulled out his firearm and began chasing Sevier, who had to hide behind a tree while their second's tried to calm them down. Eventually, Jackson was calmed down, and both men parted ways without any bloodshed. Supporters of Jackson and Sevier spent the next several months insulting each other in the papers, and debating each other in the bars. The dispute between the Governor and the Commander of the Militia helped advance Jackson's reputation as a man of principle and garnered him a lot of attention, which was important, since he was a political upstart at this time.[1]

After these two attempts Jackson would finally participate in a bona fide duel. This notorious challenge with rival horse breeder, attorney, and Southern plantation owner Charles Dickinson cemented Jackson's legendary status. Much like the duel with Sevier, Jackson's dispute with Dickinson brewed over a longer period of time, but this time it wasn't a political argument that led to blows but a disagreement over a horse race. Jackson bet Dickinson's father-in-law, Joseph Erwin, two thousand dollars that his horse could whop any horse from Erwin's stable. Erwin agreed, but before the race began Erwin's horse went lame and the race was canceled, leaving Jackson to fight with him over a forfeit penalty. An irritated Erwin paid Jackson, who stormed off to spread foul rumors about Erwin and Dickinson. These rumors forced Dickinson to send a "spy" to scour the town in hopes of learning just what exactly Jackson was saying about him. But Jackson soon discovered the spy at a local pub and pummeled him bloody with his wooden cane.

With his spy defeated, Dickinson should have learned his lesson and backed off, but instead he became more outspoken and began publishing a series of articles denouncing Jackson as a cheating coward—to which Jackson naturally replied by challenging Dickinson to a duel.

Because Dickinson was a master marksman who had already vanquished twenty-six prior opponents, he gladly accepted Jackson's offer. On May 30, 1806, Jackson and Dickinson faced off in the rising southern sun.

Running through Harrison Mills, Kentucky, the Red River flowed just as tranquilly as it had for hundreds of years—Friday, May 30, 1806, was no different. While the water ran, however, two men gathered along one of its banks just as the sun rose into the morning sky. One man arrived to dispatch a political opponent and the other to defend the honor of his wife. On the morning of Friday, May 30, 1806, the Red River was to play witness to the duel between Charles Dickinson and Andrew Jackson. Dickinson (only twenty-six years of age), who viewed the thirty-nine-year-old Jackson to be a political thorn, was encouraged to insult Jackson's wife Rachel to his face, effectively ensuring that Jackson would challenge Dickinson to a duel.

Through much of their marriage, Andrew and Rachel Jackson faced constant criticism and ill-mannered effrontery as they were married before the divorce between Rachel and her first husband became official. Jackson knew that his wife's past would become somewhat of a liability in his public and political career and, as a result, was always prepared to defend her and her honor. Before ever becoming president, Jackson fought 103 duels mostly defending the integrity of his wife. As a result, Jackson is said to have kept 37 pistols ready to be used in a duel at all times. Such was the occasion on the bank of the Red River in May of 1806.

Paces apart, Jackson and Dickinson stood opposed to one another. At a mere 24 feet from one another, many thought that Dickinson would easily shoot and kill Jackson. To make this assumption, however, would prove to be a serious misunderstanding of Jackson and his abilities. The two Tennessee men traveled to the neighboring Kentucky, as dueling was illegal in Tennessee, to settle their score. Each man held a 70-caliber pistol—a matching set—and made ready for confrontation. John Overton, a general in the military present at the duel, announced the duel should begin. Squaring himself, Dickinson aimed and fired at Jackson's heart. Despite smoke and dust billowing from Jackson's coat and his hand touching his chest, Jackson remained standing, puzzling the accomplished Dickinson. Reportedly, Dickinson asked, "My God! Have I missed him?" Nevertheless, the decorum of dueling stated that Dickinson was required to remain in place while Jackson aimed to take his shot. Jackson fired, but the flint hammer stopped half-cocked, not counting as a legitimate shot. Jackson aimed again—ever so carefully—and fired a second time. This time, the shot was good, and the bullet hit Dickinson in the chest and he dropped to the ground. Jackson was a notoriously terrible marksman and he knew if he was to be successful in this duel, he would need to remain calm and possibly take a bullet. He calculated that if he could be the one to take the second shot, he could better steady his nerves and take careful aim—he could take a better shot than Dickinson had done in haste. Dickinson would succumb to his wounds, dying later that night. Conversely, Jackson would survive, though with two broken ribs and a bullet inches from his heart that was never removed.[2]

Fig. 3.3. Andrew Jackson duels Charles Dickinson.
Presidentialmuseum.org

Jackson recovered from the duel with a bullet that rattled in his chest from time to time, and every once in a while he coughed up blood, but, according to him, he would have taken a slug in the *brain* in order to get rid of Dickinson. Years after the duel had taken place the Rothschilds tried to use this incident to thwart Jackson's presidential ambitions, claiming in their newspapers that he should be prosecuted for murder. And yet, despite this, the duel had little effect on preempting Jackson's campaign for the presidency in 1828, given that most American men of the 1800s viewed dueling as a time-honored tradition.

The newspapers then tried to turn Jackson's war-hero status against him by printing that he had ordered the executions of militia members accused of desertion. To this end, John Binns, the notorious editor of the *Philadelphia Democratic Press,* published the "coffin handbill," a poster showing six black coffins adorned with the names of the militia men Jackson had executed, despite the only proof of this being "an eye witness."

Even Jackson's forty-year frontier marriage became fodder for cam-

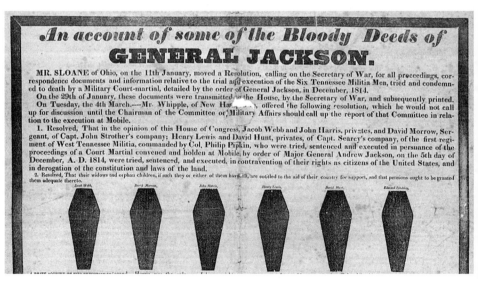

Fig. 3.4. The "coffin handbill" was published by the *Philadelphia Democratic Press* in what was one attempt of many to defame Andrew Jackson.
Virginia Historical Society

paign attacks when his wife, Rachel, and their apparently questionable marriage became embarrassing front-page news. The nation was enamored of the story of Jackson's wife, who had allegedly married Jackson while still being the wife of another man. As mentioned earlier, this called into question whether she and Jackson had lived together without Rachel having been properly divorced. Thus, Jackson was accused of adultery and criticized for running off with another man's wife, and Rachel was accused of bigamy. Jackson was furious at the assaults on them, but the public viewed the matter as little more than soap opera gossip.

When the final election tallies were counted, Jackson had won the popular vote by a landslide, and he rolled into office in 1828 with a clear and decisive victory to the utter shock of the money changers. There would be no controversy this time as Jackson's appeal to the common folk served him well, easily securing both the popular and electoral vote. However, the victory came with a price: Jackson's beloved wife, Rachel, suffered a heart attack and died before the inauguration in 1829. Jackson was livid over her death and accused his rivals of somehow being the cause.

When Jackson arrived in Washington he was all business and refused the customary courtesy call to the outgoing president, John Quincy Adams, who in turn responded by refusing to attend Jackson's inauguration, thus missing the biggest party ever thrown at the White House.

Jackson had a huge, popular following, and his inauguration was a sea change for American politics. A crowd of 10,000 to 20,000 people showed up at the Capitol for the inauguration, some traveling from 500 miles away for the event. The sight stunned Washington society and Jackson's political enemies, who already feared "mob rule" under Jackson. The sixty-one-year-old Jackson gave his inaugural address and promised to do the best job for the people . . . the president mounted his own horse, and he rode through the crowd to the White House. Another crowd was already outside and inside the mansion, as the tradition of the day made inauguration day an "open house" for the White House. In theory, anyone could show up, shake the president's hand, and maybe have some punch and dessert.

The popular story is that Jackson entered the White House, and a mob scene broke out with the rabble ransacking the White House and Jackson fleeing for safety. One source for that story was a memoir written by Margaret Bayard Smith, a Washington society figure. "But what a scene did we witness! The Majesty of the People had disappeared, and a rabble, a mob, of boys, negros [*sic*], women, children, scrambling, fighting, romping. What a pity what a pity! No arrangements had been made, no police officers placed on duty, and the whole house had been inundated by the rabble mob."

James Hamilton, Jr., a representative from South Carolina, wrote the next day to Martin Van Buren and called the event a "Saturnalia." But two historians, David and Jeanne Heidler, wrote in 2004 about other contemporary accounts that play down the drunken-brawl aspects of the open house. The Heidlers point out that Hamilton, the Jackson supporter from South Carolina, called the damage from the event "trivial." The crowd at the White House was mixed. The first arrivals were the people who made up Washington society. The second crowd that showed up at the mansion was made up of Jackson supporters who were dressed in their best clothes. What happened next doesn't seem to be disputed. The White House wasn't prepared for the crowd as it pressed in through the front door and sought out Jackson, along with the food and whiskey-laced punch. Jackson found himself pressed into a situation with his back to a wall until his people were able to get him away from the crowd, and back to his hotel. The sheer number of people inside the White House led to collisions with furniture and food.

After Jackson left, the Heidlers say Antoine Michel Giusta, the White House steward, moved the party outside by taking the punch outside. Other reports indicated that staffers passed punch and ice cream through the White House's windows to the crowd outside. As for the image of a riot of drunken Jackson supporters, the Heidlers believed that the incident was used as a metaphor by Washington society and Jackson's enemies, who feared the new regime and its lower-class roots. "Most witnesses, however, mentioned little real damage, and newspapers reported only incidental breakage. *Niles' Weekly Register,* in fact, merely observed that Jackson had 'received the salutations of a vast number of persons, who came to congratulate him upon his induction to the presidency,'" said the Heidlers.

The story about the cheese actually happened at the end of Jackson's eight years in office. The president was given a 1,400-pound cheese wheel as a gift, and it sat in the White House for several years. Finally, Jackson allowed the public into the East Room to eat the cheese, which it consumed over several days in 1837. The

Fig. 3.5. A view of the crowd in front of the White House during President Jackson's first inaugural reception in 1829. The furnishings of the White House were destroyed by the rowdy crowd during the festivities.
Illustration by Robert Cruickshank (1841)

odors lingered for days after the event. In the end, Jackson seemed unfazed by the open house incident in 1829. He had planned on redecorating the White House anyway and was able to get $50,000 from Congress for his project.[3]

The Rothschilds' worst fears would now come true as Jackson began his presidency with the intent of removing all those who favored the bankers. During his first term Jackson was successful in cleaning out the Rothschilds' many minions from government service and fired more than half of the federal government. Jackson also began an investigation of the Rothschilds' central banking headquarters located at the Second Bank of the United States. The president soon discovered that the bank was privately owned, mostly by foreign stockholders with political agendas that were not in America's favor. Two of the biggest American traitors whom Jackson targeted were Second Bank director Nicholas Biddle and Jackson's very own vice president, John C. Calhoun.

Calhoun was a slave-owning elitist who foresaw a slave-free future in his beloved South, so he advocated a movement to combat the rising antislavery sentiment that was brewing in America with an idea called states' rights. This doctrine claimed that each state had an inherent right to do whatever it wanted and could even secede from the Union if it so desired. Calhoun used this idea to rattle the South into believing it had been dealt a bad hand thanks to the high tariff taxes that had been imposed on it. Because of the tariff on foreign commodities most Southern merchants made very little on exported goods sold to Europe and were forced to buy and sell mainly from Northern competitors.

Calhoun continued to champion the ideas of states' rights, which put the liberties of men before those of the Union. However he failed to recognize that the Union was backed by the United States Constitution, a doctrine that already protected our inherent liberties. Calhoun was continuing the dirty work of the Rothschilds by putting in the public mind that the Union could be dissolved and the states soon would be battling each other for supremacy just like the nations of Europe had done throughout history. However the tariff issue died out and the dreams of Calhoun and the Rothschilds for a civil war were shelved for another thirty years. Jackson knew that Calhoun's plot was devised to destroy the United States and its constitutional liberties, and he was intent on removing him from office as soon as possible. Jackson was also dealing with his archrival Nicholas Biddle, who by 1830 was in full control of the federal government's banking system.

As Jackson was becoming a giant in the White House, more discoveries of ancient giants were being made across the new nation. In 1829, Chesterville Ohioans who were preparing to build a hotel dug through a large mound only to discover the bones of a giant. When the perplexed discoverer of the body placed the unearthed jawbone over his own he was shocked to find that it was more than double the size of his. Unfortunately the giant's jawbone and skull were lost after being taken to the nearby town of Mansfield.

Bones of large giants had been reported in upstate Rochester, New York, since the late 1700s. In 1796, on the shores of Irondequoit Bay, the destruction of a sandy mound by flood revealed a pile of giant skeletons. In *History of the Pioneer Settlement of Phelps and Gorham's Purchase, and Morris' Reserve,* published in 1851, author O. Turner confirms these claims, writing, "As late as 1830 human bones of an unusually large size were occasionally seen projecting from the face of the bluff or lying on the beach. The arm and leg bones, upon comparison, were much larger than those of our own race."[4]

Another giant discovery was made in the upstate village of North Tonawanda on the Niagara River in 1896 when the affluent businessman Stephen White and his family arrived from Manhattan. But the plot of land they had purchased had a slight problem: a much cherished icon of the Natives, a massive ten-foot-high burial mound, was standing in their way. But White didn't care about savage traditions and took a shovel to the mound. Eventually, when the mound had been destroyed, all the White family could do was scratch their heads in awe. What had been uncovered were two giant skeletons, both more than eight feet tall.[5]

In Henry Howe's *Historical Collections of Ohio* he writes about a tree marking an age of giants. This tree, which was next to an ancient pre-Columbian fort that had been dubbed "Fort Hill," had been cut down in 1829. "The Hon. Nehemiah King, with a magnifying glass, counted 350 annular rings beyond some cut marks near the tree's center. Deducting 350 from 1829, leaves 1479, which must have been the year when these cuts were made. This was 13 years before the discovery of America, by Columbus. It perhaps was done by the race of the mounds, with an axe of copper, as that people had the art of hardening that metal so as to cut like steel."[6]

Giants were once again popping up in religious writings as well thanks to the newfound popularity of the Mormon religion and the work of the Reverend Solomon Spalding of Conneaut, Ohio. Spalding was a friend of Aaron Wright, the discoverer of the Conneaut giants (referenced in chapter 2) and decided to write a historical novel based on Wright's discoveries mixed with the legends of giants that had played a huge role in the myths of the Iroquois. Spalding died before his book *Manuscript Found* was published. Some people believe that Joseph Smith, the founder of the Mormon Church, ripped off Spalding's writings and turned them into the Book of Mormon, especially the parts about the Nephi, which Smith claimed were related to pre-Columbian giants. Joseph Smith, who was the supposed translator of the "Nephite record" from which the Book of Mormon derives, mentions giants as being men of mighty or large stature only a few times throughout the book. However, this didn't stop Mormon writer E. Cecil McGavin from making the Mormon Nephites distant relatives of the Conneaut giants of upstate New York. In *Geography of the Book of Mormon* he writes:

> Cayuga County [NY] yielded a rich harvest of giant skeletons among the ancient ruins, of which we read that "entire skeletons have been found of people of giant proportions, the skulls and jawbones of which could cover the head and face of the most fleshy person of our day." We are told of a tradition which asserts that a destructive war

was waged "in this very section of the country, and with such fury and determination on each side that practically all of the warriors were slaughtered." Erie County has yielded a vast store of ancient monuments, including many giant skeletons, spear points, war hatchets, and other weapons that seem too large for an average-sized man to wield. Bones of "giant size" have been uncovered. Similar discoveries have been made in Ontario County; skeletons of an early age including many of unusual size have been found.[7]

Mormon scholars such as Charles B. Thompson identified the mound builders as the giants of the Nephite and Jaredite races. Other visionary writers described them as huge men who wore gigantic golden breastplates and wielded large copper swords. The Book of Mormon, however, is largely silent on the matter. Phyllis Carol Olive, author of *The Lost Lands of the Book of Mormon,* is convinced that the ancient mound-building culture of Ohio is directly related to the giants first spoken about in the Book of Mormon. Although the Mormons' imaginative conjectures about the giants of the Ohio Valley being related to a race of giants from the days before Jesus may be exciting and vindicating to the faithful, the truth is that giant skeletons belonging to the mound builders had been publicized long before the first copy of the Book of Mormon was ever sold.

Author David Marks reports that he was drawn to investigate the newly published Book of Mormon in 1830, due to his "curiosity" while visiting in Ohio, "to know the origin of the numerous mounds and remains of ancient fortifications that abound in that section of the country . . ." and due to his "having been told that the 'Book of Mormon' gave a history of them." Rev. Marks might have just as well said that he had a curiosity to know the origins of the numerous huge skeletons dug from those same mounds. And, in that case, Phyllis Carol Olive would have a ready answer: that they are the same as "those described in the Book of Mormon." However, since the curiosity of such investigators as David Marks pre-dated the coming forth of the Book of Mormon, how can the Mormon apologist answer the question, "Could not the book have been written to explain (among other things) the mounds and giants which had already aroused peoples' curiosity?"

In the case of Solomon Spalding's productions, the answer to that question is "Yes, of course—Spalding himself admits to that at the beginning of his story." If Solomon Spalding incorporated explanations of the prehistoric mounds, finds of huge skeletons, extinct American elephants, ancient seer-stones, and other such oddities in his 1812 book in order to satisfy the curiosity of an inquiring public, could not have some writer compiled the Book of Mormon for much the same purpose? At the very least, the fact remains that people were inquisitive about the origin of the prehistoric giant skeletons long before either book was made available to their curious readers. The modern investigator is left to conclude that *if* Solomon Spalding did write a good deal of the Book of Mormon—and *if* his supposedly purloined "Manuscript Found" story really said very much at all about ancient American giants—that the text published in 1830 must have been significantly changed from whatever it was that Spalding wrote in Ohio two decades before.[8]

Some believe that Solomon Spalding's speculations about giants may have been influenced by the discovery of large teeth and bones from an unidentified animal discovered near Albany, New York, in 1705. The poet Edward Taylor penned a few verses about this monster in which he rhymed verse about ancient Native American traditions of a prehistoric race of giants. The biblical connections were soon made by the Reverend Cotton Mather when he linked the teeth and the protruding giant bones on Irondequoit Bay to the biblical giants from the days of old. And because Solomon Spalding had lived for several years near Albany, where the giant bones were first uncovered, it's more than likely that he was familiar with Rev. Mather's theories identifying them as proof of biblical giants. However, in 1806, these purported giant bones of an ancient American race turned out to be nothing other than plain old mastodon bones.

According to reports from the 1884 *History of Erie County, Pennsylvania,* giants had been discovered in a graveyard full of dead soldiers.

> Many indications have been found in the county [Erie] proving conclusively that it was once peopled by a different race from the Indians who were found here when it was first visited by white men. When the link of the Erie & Pittsburgh Railroad from the Lake Shore road to the dock at Erie was in process of construction, the laborers dug into a great mass of bones at the crossing of the public road which runs by the rolling mill. From the promiscuous way in which they were thrown together, it is surmised that a terrible battle must have taken place in the vicinity at some day so far distant that not even a tradition of the event has been preserved. . . .
>
> At a later date . . . another deposit of bones was dug up. . . . Among the skeletons was one of a giant, side by side with a smaller one, probably that of his wife. The arm and leg bones of this native American Goliath were about one-half longer than those of the tallest man among the laborers; the skull was immensely large, the lower jaw-bone easily slipped over the face and whiskers of a full-faced man, and the teeth were in a perfect state of preservation. Another skeleton was dug up in Conneaut Township some years ago which was quite remarkable in its dimensions. As in the other instance, a comparison was made with the largest man in the neighborhood, and the jawbone readily covered his face, while the lower bone of the leg was nearly a foot longer than the one with which it was measured, indicating that the man must have been eight to ten feet in height.[9]

Township histories that discuss giants and ancient mounds and date back to the days when Solomon Spalding was living within the

Fig. 3.6. The ten-foot-tall giants found in a cave in Erie County, Pennsylvania.
Gianthumanskeletons.blogspot.com

vicinity may prove that a great deal of his thinking and writing was influenced by these stories. The *Jefferson Gazette* of Ashtabula County, Ohio, cleared up the Mormon giant matter in 1924.

The early settlers of Ashtabula have gone on record that where the east side cemetery is there were over 1000 graves when they came here, laid out with some evidence of mathematical skill. A few graves were opened and in some were found skulls and jaw bones of men whose size dwarfed the men who found the graves. The graves were not those of the Indian of the last or the previous century. . . . In the early days settlers in Conneaut found a number of mounds. On the west side along the creek there was a great burial ground. It is said there were about 3000 graves there, laid out in some design and like the cemetery at Ashtabula the bones of the adults were exceptionally large. . . .

One of the most interesting stories arising from the old burial plot at Conneaut was the probable origin of the Book of Mormon. . . . Rev. Spalding, in about 1812 . . . told that he found [a] manuscript in one of the old graves at Conneaut. . . . A few years later it was uncovered by Sidney Rigdon, a preacher from Kirtland, Ohio, who had been prophesying that a great revelation was about to be made the chosen people at Kirtland. Rigdon conspired with Smith, father of Mormonism, to find the manuscript, which Smith did . . . from this scheme and the old Spalding fraud may have come, and probably did come, the formation of the present great Mormon church of Utah.[10]

Why have accounts of these giants been whitewashed from America's history books? As was discussed extensively in our previous book, *The Suppressed History of America,* the early government of the United States was intent on ensuring that Indians were removed from the American landscape in order to encourage settlers to expand westward. To this end, the Smithsonian Institution was deemed to be the arbiter of cultural knowledge, the gatekeepers if you will of historical facts about our great country. It actively manipulated the version of history that reached the public, and then it codified it. To confirm that giants had once roamed America would be to contribute to the idea of their dominance in the American landscape and could be a deterrent to settlement. Thus these accounts were obliterated from the official record.

This sanctioning was part and parcel of America's formative strategy for growth as a nation, part of which was to throw off all forms of European domination as America struggled to find its own, brand-new identity that had nothing to do with other cultures or other races. We see this shucking of foreign domination in Jackson's repulsion for the

Rothschilds and their machinations to establish and continually recharter a central bank, which would be owned by foreign investors acting like leeches on the American financial system.

While many more giants of the Ohio Valley rested underneath unopened mounds waiting to be discovered, Andrew Jackson was preparing to be reelected president in 1832. Knowing that the Rothschilds' charter for their central banking scheme would run out in 1836, Jackson ran full steam ahead with his election campaign aimed at killing the banks. For Jackson to successfully accomplish this, he would have to be reelected president and survive until the last year of his presidency, when the charter expired. Jackson was hell bent on killing the banks and once and for all dispensing with the Rothschilds' prized pupil, Nicholas Biddle.

Fearing the worst, the Rothschilds prepared to pull out all the stops to maintain control of the American economy. The real struggle for the future of America was about to be waged, and as Jackson prepared to do battle with the seven-headed Hydra the odds were against him once more. But Jackson was a determined individual who loved a good scrap, and if anybody was going to be the one to defeat the Rothschilds it was going to be him—if he could survive long enough to do it.

4
Battling the Seven-Headed Hydra

1832–1835

Pastime Paradise

They've been spending most their lives
Living in a pastime paradise
They've been wasting most their time
Glorifying days long gone behind
Tell me who of them will come to be
How many of them are you and me
Dissipation
Race relations
Consolation
Segregation
Dispensation
Isolation
Exploitation
Mutilation
Mutations
Miscreation
Confirmation, to the evils of the world

STEVIE WONDER

The victor will never be asked if he told the truth.

ADOLF HITLER

Andrew Jackson was ready for the election of 1832, unique in its time given that it was the first example of parties holding nominating conventions. Also for the first time, the election of 1832 introduced a third party for which to vote—the Anti-Masonic Party. Thus, three nominees were running for president that year. They included the front-runner and current man in charge, Andrew Jackson (Democrat); a member of the Anti-Masonic party William Wirt; and the Republican representative Henry Clay.

Clay was known as "the great compromiser" and had served in Congress for more than thirty years before deciding to run for president. He had been instrumental in getting John Quincy Adams elected president in 1824 and was rewarded with the post of secretary of state shortly thereafter. This confirmation was proof to Jackson that the presidential election was a corrupt bargain and was essentially rigged.

Clay was a central banking advocate who was viewed by Jackson as being untrustworthy and opportunistic. And despite Clay's moniker, "the great compromiser," Jackson believed that Clay would do *anything* without compromise to advance his own self-serving objectives. Jackson's beef with Clay stemmed from 1819 at least, when Clay admonished Jackson before Congress for the general's unauthorized invasion of Spanish Florida in 1818. Clay's strategic vision for America relied on loans to the federal government from the central bank. These loans would fund public works programs like federally funded road and canal improvements. But Jackson believed the propositions to be unconstitutional (could federal funds be used to build roads?) and vetoed the projects. They included the Maysville Road Bill, which was Clay's final attempt at gaining federal funds for transportation improvements.

Clay was entering into the upcoming election with a good idea of how he wanted the country to be run, and Jackson knew that Clay's ideas and plans were designed to benefit from the vast amount of resources that would be culled from the central bank. Jackson had defeated Clay in the 1832 election, but now with the Second Bank's charter coming up for renewal in four years he feared the Rothschilds would sink an ungodly sum of money into Clay's campaign.

It was bad enough that Clay was friends with his vice president, John C. Calhoun, a man who had turned into a bitter rival of Jackson's during the president's first year in office. Jackson scored a personal victory, however, when Calhoun became the first vice president to resign, allowing Jackson's friend Martin Van Buren to join him in Calhoun's stead. Calhoun immediately joined the Senate, where he led the proslavery and secession movements.

Jackson's other competitor in the 1832 election was William Wirt, a member of the Anti-Masonic Party, attorney general, prolific writer of letters, and close friend of Thomas Jefferson. Wirt had been a former Freemason but quit the organization after obtaining only his first two degrees. (His Masonic cult status would peak unexpectedly in the 1970s, when members of the infamous Skull and Bones society broke into his tomb and stole his skull for an occult ritual.)

The presence of the Anti-Masonic Party in the election of 1832 was a great help to Jackson's campaign, because it pulled votes away from the Republicans. This new party was the first "third party" movement to successfully emerge and put forth a viable candidate who opposed the traditional power structures that ran the government. It even introduced nominating conventions and party platforms, which were two important innovations to American politics.

Members of the Anti-Masonic Party greatly opposed Freemasonry and viewed it as a satanic force of corruption steering America in the wrong direction. They publically associated the occult and secret practices of the Freemasons with the Illuminati, and in so doing they hoped to bring more public awareness to the issues of corruption within the government. They were basically right in the names of the Masons and members of the Illuminati in the halls of government and in prominent civilian operations whom they exposed. Because so many judges, businessmen, bankers, and politicians were often Masons the general public began to think of them as an elitist group who were bound by secret oaths and biased toward outsiders.

Thus, despite the good intentions of members of the Anti-Masonic Party, their run had the opposite effect, and they folded as an organization a few years after the election. Wirt himself would also die a few years after the contest. The fever they had stirred up in the press against the Masons was only detrimental to mostly regular "Porch" Masons, who were persecuted while the real power players like Nicholas Biddle and those doing the dirty deeds for the Rothschilds were left untouched, most likely due to the fact that they could never be tied to anything as trivial as joining a lodge. Conspiracy theories about shady government dealings were just as common back then as they are today. At least the Anti-Masonic Party tried to do something about it.

The Masons had a bad reputation in 1832, which was due in part to the fact that most of the nation was still upset about the dreaded Morgan affair, wherein the public was convinced that the Masons had murdered the 33rd degree former Mason William Morgan for speaking out against them and threatening to expose their secrets in a book he was writing, which was titled *Illustrations of Masonry*. Morgan, a former captain who served in the War of 1812 was rumored to have been drowned in Niagara Lake by the Masons in 1826. How he died is still up for debate; all we know for sure is that Morgan disappeared off the face of the Earth. His book would be published posthumously to critical acclaim.

From beyond the grave Morgan became a champion of free speech and freedom of the press. His story inspired the rise of the Anti-Masonic Party and its run for the White House. This party was even outspoken against Andrew Jackson and attacked him on the grounds that he was a high-ranking Freemason just like all the prior presidents had been. Despite Jackson's valiant war record, the Anti-Masonic Party didn't see him as a man of the people but rather as another slave-owning Freemason elitist. This Masonic bashing of Jackson might have come as a surprise to a few people, but to most Americans his dabbling in Masonry wasn't as relevant as his commendable record against the

British in New Orleans, against the Indians in the Southeast, and against the central bank in the North.

Jackson *was* a Mason; he even claimed that "Freemasonry is an institution calculated to benefit mankind," as recorded in the *Freemasons' Quarterly,* but he was also a man who owed his salvation and fortune to slave trading. At one point in his life Jackson had more than 150 slaves working for him on various plantations that he owned throughout the South. He was quite unlike Robert Carter III, the inheritor of a wealthy estate in Virginia who, in 1791, emancipated all of his five hundred slaves, which is to this day the largest number of slaves emancipated by an individual slave owner in the history of the United States.

Jackson bought his first slave in 1788 and continued to own them his entire life. Even after he died Jackson refused to free any of his slaves in his will. Jackson was also responsible for the death of thousands of Native Americans, thanks to a law he enacted known as the Indian Removal Act, which basically legalized the ethnic cleansing of the Native peoples of America. By 1837 more than forty-six thousand indigenous people had been shuffled from their homelands east of the Mississippi, leaving their twenty-five million acres of land in the hands of white settlers and slave owners. By the time he was up for reelection, Jackson was already a proud, high-ranking Mason who frequently spoke in praise of the organization. The following excerpt is from the 1957 book *10,000 Famous Freemasons* by William R. Denslow.

Masonic History of Andrew Jackson (1767–1845), Seventh President of the United States. b. March 15, 1767, in Washaw settlement between North and South Carolina. He was admitted to the bar in Salisbury, N.C. in 1787, and, the following year, migrated westward to Nashville, Tenn. Here he became a U.S. congressman (1796–97); U.S. senator (1797–98); judge of the Tenn. Supreme Court (1798–1804); and major general of Tennessee militia (1802). He defeated the Creek Indians at the Battle of Horseshoe Bend in 1814, and was made major general of United States Army and assigned to defend New Orleans in the

War of 1812. His defense of that city made him a national hero. He added to his fame by operations against the Seminole Indians in 1818, and involved the federal government by pursuing Indians into Spanish territory, and hanging two English troublemakers. He was governor of the Florida Territory in 1821, and again U.S. senator in 1823–25. His first presidential race in 1824 was unsuccessful, but he was elected in 1828, and reelected in 1832. . . .

There is doubt as to when and where he received his degrees. An article in *The Builder* in 1925 states, "The claim of Greeneville Lodge No. 3 of Tenn. (formerly No. 43 of N.C.) seems to be the most weighty. An original transcript shows that he (Jackson) was a member at that time." W. L. Boydon wrote in the *New Age* in Aug. 1920, "The generally accepted belief is that he was made a Mason in Philanthropic Lodge No. 12 at Clover Bottom, Davidson Co., Tenn." Bell, in his *Famous Masons,* states, "Jackson was a member of Harmony Lodge No. 1 (formerly St. Tammany Lodge No. 29 of N.C.) Nashville, as early as 1800, but the date of receiving the degrees has not been learned. He was present at the first meeting of Tennessee Lodge No. 2, Knoxville, March 24, 1800." Charles Comstock, past Grand Master of Tennessee and historian, believes that he was a member of Harmony Lodge and records a visit by him to the initial meeting of Polk Lodge, U.D.1 Knoxville (dispensation granted Jan. 15, 1800), by "Andrew Jackson of Harmony Lodge of Nashville." In 1808, Harmony Lodge No. 1 lost its charter, and here all record of Jackson's Masonic affiliation ceases until 1822. He evidently kept in good standing by paying his dues to the Grand Lodge, as was then permitted. The proceedings of 1822 credit him with being a past master, but no record has been found of his mastership. He was elected Grand Master of the Grand Lodge of Tennessee, on October 7, 1822, and again in 1823, serving until October 1824. He was elected an honorary member of Federal Lodge No. 1, Washington, D.C., January 4, 1830, and of Jackson Lodge No. 1, Tallahassee, Fla., as well as the Grand Lodge of Florida (Jan. 15, 1833). He was a Royal

Arch Mason, as he served the Grand Chapter of Tennessee as Deputy Grand High Priest at its institution, April 3, 1826, but no record exists of his affiliation with any chapter. As was the custom at the time, the Royal Arch degree was probably conferred by a blue lodge.

He contributed $35.00 in 1818 to the erection of a Masonic temple in Nashville, requested two lodges to perform funeral services, introduced Lafayette to the Grand Lodge of Tennessee in 1825, while president assisted Washington's mother lodge to lay a cornerstone of a monument to Washington's mother in Fredericksburg, Va. (May 6, 1833), assisted in the Masonic laying of the cornerstone of Jackson City (across the river from Washington, D.C.) on January 11, 1836, attended the Grand Lodge of Tennessee in 1839, and the same year visited Cumberland Chapter No. 1 of Nashville.[1]

Jackson was an astonishing individual and one who was first in many things. Among his many "firsts," Andrew Jackson was the first American president to be the target of an assassination attempt (which

Fig. 4.1. Cotton growing at Andrew Jackson's plantation, the Hermitage, in Tennessee. Photo by Bill Carey

we will detail a little later in this chapter). In addition, Jackson was the first president to kill a man in a duel, the first "frontier" president not from the nation's elite East Coast families, the first president to ride a train, the first president who was a prisoner of war, the first president born in a log cabin, the first president to spend his inauguration night at Gadsby's Tavern, the first president to invite the public to eat at the White House, and many other firsts too numerous to list here.

Despite being a slave-owning Mason, Jackson was a beloved man of the people who had fascinated the public with his campaign promise of "killing the bank," which was a direct threat to Biddle and his central banking colleagues. As the election peaked the central banking issue became the main talking point and served as a referendum for Jackson, ending the Rothschilds' rule over the American economy.

On July 4, 1832, Congress passed a bill to extend the central banking charter another fifteen years. To Jackson the bill's timing on a much celebrated day confirmed his suspicions about the Second Bank deliberately interfering in the political process. His nemesis Nicholas Biddle backed Henry Clay, who had helped to get the recharter passed. Biddle, via the central bank, poured more than three million dollars into Clay's election campaign; a mind-boggling sum for those times. But Jackson vetoed the recharter and made it known to the public that the majority owners of the bank were in fact foreign (Rothschild) stockholders. Jackson warned in a letter to the Senate on July 10, 1832, that "if we must have a bank, it should be purely American." This fiery letter to Congress, Biddle, and the American people broke down the pitfalls and realities of the central banking/Federal Reserve system. The initial section of Jackson's response to the Second Bank's attempted rechartering is reprinted below; the letter in its entirety is found in the appendix.

To the Senate:

The bill "to modify and continue" the act entitled "An act to incorporate the subscribers to the Bank of the United States" was presented to me on the 4th July instant. Having considered it with that solemn regard to the principles of the Constitution which the day was calculated to inspire, and come to the conclusion that it ought not to become a law, I herewith return it to the Senate, in which it originated, with my objections. A bank of the United States is in many respects convenient for the Government and useful to the people. Entertaining this opinion, and deeply impressed with the belief that some of the powers and privileges possessed by the existing bank are unauthorized by the Constitution, subversive of the rights of the States, and dangerous to the liberties of the people, I felt it my duty at an early period of my Administration to call the attention of Congress to the practicability of organizing an institution combining all its advantages and obviating these objections. I sincerely regret that in the act before me I can perceive none of those modifications of the bank charter which are necessary, in my opinion, to make it compatible with justice, with sound policy, or with the Constitution of our country.

The present corporate body, denominated the president, directors, and company of the Bank of the United States, will have existed at the time this act is intended to take effect twenty years. It enjoys an exclusive privilege of banking under the authority of the General Government, a monopoly of its favor and support, and, as a necessary consequence, almost a monopoly of the foreign and domestic exchange. The powers, privileges, and favors bestowed upon it in the original charter, by increasing the value of the stock far above its par value, operated as a gratuity of many millions to the stockholders.

An apology may be found for the failure to guard against this result in the consideration that the effect of the original act of incorporation could not be certainly foreseen at the time of its passage. The act before me proposes another gratuity to the holders of the same stock, and in many cases to the same men, of at least seven millions more. This donation finds no apology in any uncertainty as to the effect of the act. On all hands it is conceded that its passage will increase at least 50 or 30 percent more the market price of the stock, subject to the payment of the annuity of $200,000 per year secured by the act, thus adding in a moment one-fourth to its par value. It is not our own citizens only who are to receive the bounty of our Government. More than eight million of the stocks of this bank are held by foreigners. By this act the American Republic proposes virtually to make them a present of some millions of dollars. For these gratuities to foreigners and to some of our own opulent citizens the act secures no equivalent whatever. They are the certain gains of the present stockholders under the operation of this act, after making full allowance for the payment of the bonus.

Every monopoly and all exclusive privileges are granted at the expense of the public, which ought to receive a fair equivalent. The many millions which this act proposes to bestow on the stockholders of the existing bank must come directly or indirectly out of the earnings of the American people. It is due to them, therefore, if their Government sells monopolies and exclusive privileges, that they should at least exact for them as much as they are worth in open market. The value of the monopoly in this case may be correctly ascertained. The twenty-eight million of stocks would probably be at an advance of 50 percent, and command in market at least $42,000,000, subject to the payment of the present bonus. The present value of the monopoly, therefore, is $17,000,000, and this act proposes to sell for three millions, payable in fifteen annual installments of $200,000 each.

It is not conceivable how the present stockholders can have any claim to the special favor of the Government. The present corporation has enjoyed its monopoly during the period stipulated in the original contract. If we must have such a corporation, why should not the Government sell out the whole stock and thus secure to the people the full market value of the privileges granted? Why should not Congress create and sell twenty-eight million of stocks, incorporating the purchasers with all the powers and privileges secured in this act and putting the premium upon the sales into the Treasury?[2]

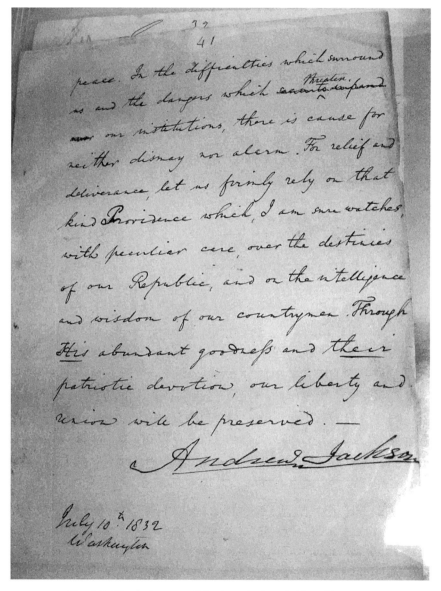

Fig. 4.2. The last page of Andrew Jackson's Veto Message.
National Archives

In all of the other presidential campaign messages, inaugurals, annuals, and vetoes that had come before, there had been nothing like this. This was an unfiltered warning to the American people about the dangers lurking in their own government, which had been corrupted and infiltrated by foreign investors. Biddle threatened that Jackson would pay for making the Second Bank a party question and published more than thirty thousand copies of his Veto Message, which he had distributed along Clay's campaign trail in the hopes that Jackson's words would be seen as inflammatory, irresponsible, and capable of inciting chaos.

Jackson responded to this by printing brochures that compared the Veto Message to the Declaration of Independence and by calling Biddle's institution "a gambler's bank." Jackson then took to the streets and won over the people with fireworks, barbecues, and parades, all of which had a much more positive effect on the public than the newspapers, posters, and brochures had. Jackson then formed an allegiance with working-class farmers, mechanics, and laborers and campaigned with his slogan "Jackson and No Bank" against rich and powerful elite capitalists. In so doing he easily earned the support of the people, who reelected him president in a landslide victory, much to the dismay of Biddle and his Rothschild backers.

However, Jackson knew the battle with Biddle was just beginning, and following his victory he told James K. Polk, "The hydra of corruption is only scotched, not dead."[3] He then ordered his new secretary of the Treasury, Lewis McClean, to start removing the government's deposits from Biddle's Second Bank and to start placing them in state banks. But McClean refused to do so and was instantly fired by Jackson, who replaced him with William J. Duane. But Duane was also a Biddle stooge and refused to comply with Jackson's requests, and so he ended up being fired as well. It was 1833, and the bank war was on full bore as Jackson desperately sought allies to help him kick out the Rothschild-dominated Second Bank.

He finally got the help he needed when former attorney general

Roger Taney stepped up to be secretary of the Treasury. Taney would help Jackson in his fight against the bank. However, although he was all for battling a central banking system, when it came to slavery Taney was a staunch admirer of the practice and had no intention of giving it up. In this respect it makes sense that he would be best remembered for the embarrassing Dred Scott decision.

In *Dred Scott v. Sandford,* an African-American slave named Dred Scott had appealed to the Supreme Court in hopes of being granted his freedom based on his having been brought by his masters to live in free territories. The Taney Court ruled that persons of African descent could not be, nor were ever intended to be, citizens under the U.S. Constitution, and thus the plaintiff (Scott) was without legal standing to file a suit. The framers of the Constitution, Taney famously wrote, believed that blacks "had no rights which the white man was bound to respect; and that the negro might justly and lawfully be reduced to slavery for his benefit. He was bought and sold and treated as an ordinary article of merchandise and traffic, whenever profit could be made by it." The court also declared the Missouri Compromise (1820) unconstitutional, thus permitting slavery in all of the country's territories. Taney died during the final months of the American Civil War on the same day that his home state of Maryland abolished slavery.[4]

On October 1, 1833, Jackson announced that federal funds would no longer be deposited in the Second Bank of the United States and instead instructed Taney to begin placing them in twenty-three various state-chartered banks. Taney, on the orders of Jackson, began withdrawing government funds from the Second Bank. To do this Jackson had the bank's status changed so that it would no longer have any financial ties with the government. This resulted in a crippling lack of funds for the bank, which now was left out in the cold as Jackson took complete control of the government.

Fig. 4.3. Anti-Jackson poster shows Andrew Jackson as a monarch trampling the Constitution, the federal judiciary, and the Bank of the United States.

Jackson and Taney were the only men in the entire cabinet who supported the measure. The rest vehemently opposed such a radical tactic. Jackson didn't care; he knew what he was doing and also knew that

Fig. 4.4. A Democratic cartoon showing Jackson destroying the bank with his "Order of Removal," to the approval of the Uncle Sam–like figure to the right and the annoyance of the bank's president, shown as the devil himself. Numerous politicians and editors were given favorable loans from the bank for cover as the financial temple crashed down. Lithograph by Edward W. Clay (1833)

time was short. He told the influential journalist and politician Francis P. Blair that Biddle wouldn't be allowed to continue using public money to support the goals of Britain and other foreign banking interests. With Taney's help Jackson fired the first shots in the bank war, and Jackson's "experiment" got under way as Rothschild-owned national banking deposits were allocated to Jackson-approved state banks.

This redistribution of money to the state banks annoyed Biddle so much that he threatened to cause a depression if the Second Bank wasn't rechartered and the money that had been taken from it was not immediately replaced. It was game on for Biddle, who boldly declared, "This worthy President thinks that because he has scalped Indians and imprisoned Judges, he is to have his way with the Bank. He is

Fig. 4.5. A prizefight between Andrew Jackson and Nicholas Biddle symbolizes their struggle over the bank of the United States in this lithograph titled *Set to Between Old Hickory and Bully Nick*, engraved by Anthony Imbert, New York (1834). Courtesy of the Political Cartoon Collection, American Antiquarian Society, Worcester, Massachusetts; Common-place.org

mistaken."[5] The Second Bank's president, Nicholas Biddle, began his counteroffensive by calling in loans and restricting lines of credit. A quick little financial crisis, he reasoned, would underscore the need for the central bank's rechartering.

The people were hit with the first real blow of the bank war as a financial recession began to creep through the cities of the nation in 1834. The bank war and its chilling side effects became the talk of the town as Congress, the press, and the public furiously debated who was right and who was wrong. Scores of businessmen journeyed to Washington to complain about working conditions and the miserable

Fig. 4.6. *General Jackson Slaying the Many-Headed Monster.*
Historyhub.us

economy. Jackson welcomed them with open arms, for to him they were proof that Biddle's ability to disrupt the economy any time he wanted to only proved how dangerous the central bank was.

But Biddle stood firm as he attempted to turn Congress against Jackson by demanding that all existing loans be repaid immediately. Biddle then put a squeeze on lending, and in the fall of 1834 the central bank announced that it wasn't going to issue any new loans. This, of course, made for a rough Christmas that year as a nationwide recession hit the public hard. Biddle's ego got the best of him as both Congress and the people turned against him. His actions of curtailing loans and causing panic in the business world was intended to force the rechartering of the Second Bank, but instead Biddle discredited the bank, which reinforced Jackson's warnings of its dangerous powers.

Jackson was still at war with another old nemesis, Henry Clay, who had created a new team in the Senate called the Whigs. This Senate became the first Senate to ever formally censure a president. Jackson was steps away from being impeached, given that the Senate was furious that he had fired two Treasury secretaries for what they saw as no reason and removed government funds from the central bank. But Jackson claimed that he was in the right, based on the laws of the Constitution, and the Whigs were unable to stop him from continuing to pad his "pet banks" with Rothschild currency.

In retaliation for Congress's failed punishing of Jackson, Biddle made money so scarce that the recession turned into a depression and civil unrest began to descend upon America in the spring of 1835. This was a sight that pleased Biddle as he announced, "Nothing but widespread suffering will produce any effect on Congress. . . . Our only safety is in pursuing a steady course of firm restriction—and I have no doubt that such a course will ultimately lead to restoration of the currency and the recharter of the Bank."[6] This was a stunning revelation by one of the masters of the financial world—a polished jewel of truth revealed with shocking lucidity.

Once again the people suffered the consequences of the bank war as Biddle made good on his threat and contracted the money supply. Blaming the depression on Jackson for withdrawing federal funds from the bank, Biddle gloated as he watched wages drop, unemployment soar, foreclosures and bankruptcies boom, and inflation skyrocket. The nation went into an uproar as newspaper editors criticized Jackson as a thief and a traitor responsible for the crises. Congress was assembled in an emergency meeting to discuss what to do about the depression and the disastrous bank war.

All they could try to do was muster enough votes to override Jackson's veto so that the bank would be granted another two-decade monopoly over America's money. But this vote couldn't even get under way, because the governor of Pennsylvania stepped up in support of Jackson, claiming that at a dinner party he had overheard Biddle bragging about the bank's plan to crash the economy.

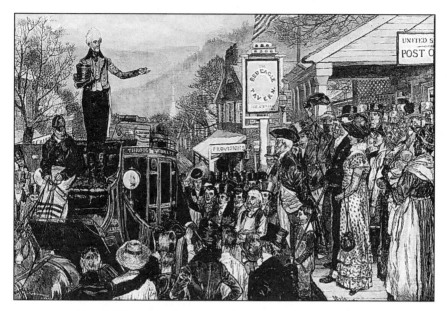

Fig. 4.7. President Jackson on his way to the emergency
meeting in Washington. Tennessee State Archives

With the realization that the bank might not actually get rechartered, Biddle and the Rothschilds began to panic. At this point they did what they always did best—they grabbed an ace from up their sleeve. When their backs were against the wall the Rothschilds never hesitated to go the extra mile, usually in the form of an assassination attempt.

A good public execution was their favorite method of sending a message. But President Jackson had a sixth sense about it and declared in a letter to Vice President Van Buren, "The bank is trying to kill me—but I will kill it!"[7] He would prove to be prophetic on both accounts. This assassination attempt is crucial to understanding just how determined the Rothschilds were to maintain control of America's money system.

The Rothschild family hired a mentally unstable and unemployed house painter named Richard Lawrence to do the deed. On a damp windy night in 1835, Lawrence approached Jackson near the steps of the Capitol building, pulled out his pistol, and shot at him, but his gun miraculously misfired. A frantic sixty-seven-year-old Jackson confronted the befuddled would-be assassin and clubbed Lawrence to the ground

Fig. 4.8. Richard Lawrence's attempt on Jackson's life,
as depicted in an 1835 etching

Fig. 4.9. The assassination attempt on Jackson's life

SCENE AT THE CAPITOL.

Fig. 4.10. *Scene at the Capitol* from "Shooting at the President! The Remarkable Trial of Richard Lawrence, for an Attempt to Assassinate the President of the United States," by a Washington reporter (1835). W. Mitchell

with his cane. Lawrence, shielding his face with his arms and still scuffling with Jackson, managed to pull out a *second* loaded pistol, aiming at Jackson's stomach. He pulled the trigger, but it also misfired. Jackson glowed as if surrounded by a mystical halo that was impervious to bullets; Lawrence was dumbfounded and was soon wrestled into submission and captured by Jackson's aides.

Jackson was unharmed, surviving an assassination attempt wherein two pistols somehow managed to misfire in a more than one hundred twenty-five thousand to one chance of that ever happening. Later, in true vainglorious fashion, Jackson erected a statue of himself at the site of the assassination attempt. Lawrence pleaded not guilty by reason of insanity and was sentenced to remain in a mental institution for the rest of his life. Lawrence would rot away and die in the mental ward but not before admitting that powerful people from England had hired him to kill the president.

Jackson had survived, and, given that the bank's charter was set to expire in a year, he looked forward to 1836 when he could finally stick his bowie knife in the gut of the bank. But as usual the Rothschilds were looking to the future; they had acquired the rights to the Almadén quicksilver mines in Spain. Quicksilver was utilized in the minting of coins. Acquiring this mine gave the Rothschilds the edge in the refinement of gold and silver and ensured them a global economic monopoly. They soon began refining gold and silver for the Royal Mint, the Bank of England, and other international monetary institutions. The Rothschilds were sewing up control over Europe, but back in America their vice grip was loosening. Their main man, Nicholas Biddle, had thus far been unsuccessful in removing Jackson from the equation, and as 1836 loomed the prospects for their continued economic dominance in America looked grim.

Jackson, on the other hand, was confident that he had made all the right moves, and, despite being paranoid after surviving an assassination attempt, his confidence in destroying the bank and Biddle was at an all-time high. He was in the process of eliminating the national debt and putting the central bank out of business, and as 1836 got under way he prepared for things to get even crazier. Heading into the final rounds of his battle with the seven-headed Hydra, Jackson declared that the den of vipers and all those housed within it would be routed out of Washington. It was a promise Jackson made good on as 1836 became a year to remember for him and a year that Nicholas Biddle and the Rothschilds would never forget.

5
Jackson Kills the Bank

1836–1846

Movie of Life

Economies come crashing down
But money's silent when it hits the ground
What you hear is panic and fear
spreadin' through the atmosphere
Bankster scams try to save
their House of Cards
built by paper slaves
And they rob the world
of all you own
While everybody's lookin'
at their cell phone
The BRICS, the mortar, the New World Order
False Flags, global warming,
shuttin' down the border
MK Ultra trying to puncture
the fragile psychic thread
of the human culture
And the only people cheering
Genetic Engineering
are the greedy rich

ELLIOT MERLES

I killed the bank.

ANDREW JACKSON

By the spring of 1835, Jackson had paid off the final installment on the national debt, which had been created by allowing the banks to issue currency for government bonds instead of issuing debt-free Treasury notes. With this fatal blow Andrew Jackson became the only president to ever pay off the national debt. As discussed in the previous chapter, he was rewarded for this feat by being a target for assassination a few weeks later. But the first attempt to kill a sitting American president magically failed, and the Rothschilds were left once again with cold feet in the war against their greatest foe. It would soon be 1836, and the doors to the Second Bank were about to be closed and locked forever. The recession was over, and business was again booming thanks to Jackson's state banks, which were free of Biddle's restraints and faced little regulation, freely loaning paper money to nearly anyone. Historian Fon Wyman Boardman explains:

> Jackson and the Democrats favored a policy that made land available easily and cheaply. This contradicted the hard money policy because it called for cheaper money and expansion of credit so that those with little or no savings could take up enough acreage for a self-sufficient farm. In addition, the more liberal the policy, the more it encouraged speculators to buy up large tracts and hold them until they rose in value. The common people—farmers, mechanics, and laborers—favored the Jacksonian policy. Manufacturing interests wanted a stricter policy so that the labor supply would not be decreased, thereby raising wages. Not nearly as many urban workers went to buy public lands as was once supposed. Most of those who went west to farm were already farmers, or sons of farmers, seeking their own homesteads, or, increasingly, emigrants from Europe.[1]

Financial historian Margaret G. Myers adds, "By June 1836 thirty-three banks were being used as depositaries. The new secretary of the Treasury, Levi Woodbury, urged them to build up their specie reserve and to curtail their issue of small notes, but had no way of enforcing his request unless he withdrew the deposits altogether. Both the president and the secretary professed to be delighted with the manner in which the banks were handling Treasury funds and making transfer from one part of the country to another."[2]

The economy boomed through 1836. Historian Reginald Charles McGrane tells us that

> by the spring of 1835 the country apparently had forgotten its past disorders. The price of cotton rose from 11 cents a pound in 1834 to 16 cents a pound in 1835. The quantity of public lands sold in 1835 was three times the amount of 1834. Not only was the United States out of debt, but largely through this amazing sale of the public domain, she was piling up a surplus in her treasury. The value of property in New York was higher than it had been for five years, business was brisk, and the city assumed a new aspect.[3]

But problems regarding speculation weighed heavily on Jackson's mind while the stage was being set for a major economic tightening. Congress began sticking their noses in the affair with the Act to Regulate the Deposits of Public Money, a disruptive measure meant to slow down Jackson's attempt to make $328 million of federal surplus dollars available for distribution. But the paper money was flowing, and the people were happy. This of course meant that rampant speculation on land and all other types of commodities soon followed. To combat this Jackson issued the Specie Circular on July 11, 1836. This was an executive order stating that federal land could no longer be bought with paper money but only with specie (minted coins) made of gold or silver. Jackson believed that hard physical money was the only currency one could trust.

However, this had the opposite effect Jackson had hoped for as land speculation dried up due to a lack of payments in gold or silver. There was plenty of cash and credit but not nearly enough specie. The limitations imposed by the Specie Circular forced people to buy specie at higher prices from the banks; this specie would now be the same gold or silver needed to buy land. When land sales in the West tapered off, the loss of income to state governments was crippling, making life in the West more difficult than ever before. The money situation was getting complex everywhere as higher interest rates in England forced the price of cotton way down, making Southern farmers leery of expanding operations west.

The cost of land had already quadrupled by 1836, but the receipts for these lands had largely been issued by irresponsible banks. Land speculators were forming banks with the hope that their bank would be anointed a deposit bank that could issue notes, so they could borrow them and buy land and continue to borrow the deposited notes to continue buying land indefinitely. This was a scheme that the preexisting deposit banks had a hard time fighting.

Although the West was flooded with paper money there was very little specie there. The trouble and expense it took to transport specie from the East and the desire to keep most of it in the Northeast to fight other Rothschild banks in the area alienated the West. And because the Rothschilds still controlled most of the specie in Europe, Jackson's banks would be getting none of it without a great fall in price. England was also dealing with civil unrest and unhappy citizens thanks to the speculative period that was coming to an end there, which resulted in a failing economy.

The specie reserves in banks in New York City went from $7.2 million on September 1, 1836, to $2.8 million by March 1, 1837, and to a mere $1.5 million by May, leaving the banks vulnerable to specie calls from English bankers determined to settle international balances. Scholar Richard H. Timberlake Jr. argues:

> The Specie Circular was dramatic but innocuous. The effect of the distribution was appreciable primarily, and almost entirely, because a small portion of it was a quasi-increase in the demand for hand-to-hand specie by the state governments, a demand that had to be fulfilled by the commercial banking system. Since commercial banking

systems operate on a fractional reserve basis, a decline of their specie holdings forced a manifold contraction of their demand liabilities, the medium used by the general public for conducting all its purchases and sales.[4]

Jackson's Specie Circular was notable for being his only administrative act that was consistent with the hard-money principles instilled in him as a result of his agrarian background. It was an attempt to bless America with a progressive and metallic-based economy like Europe had had in the Middle Ages. But first it was meant to weed out and prevent all of the fraud, speculation, and land-grab monopolies that arose from excessive bank credit. Ironically, Jackson's opposition to national investments in internal improvements didn't carry over to the funding of projects by state governments that ultimately lacked the resources to pay for them. Pulitzer Prize–winning professor of history Walter A. McDougall explains:

> Jackson's scruples about states' rights did not permit him to countenance a federal surplus. Accordingly, Jackson sponsored the Distribution Act of June 1836 authorizing the Treasury to lend the surplus to state governments promoting internal improvements. All that did was to encourage boosters in Indiana, Illinois, and elsewhere to launch impossibly ambitious canal and railroad projects. It almost goes without saying that the loans were never repaid. Jackson also worried about homesteaders being seduced into debt. Accordingly, he ordered the Treasury to issue a specie circular requiring that public lands be bought with hard money. All that did was to make cash-poor farmers more dependent on capital-rich speculators, magnify the fraud the president meant to expunge, and oblige his loyalists to fight little "bank wars" in every state of the Union.[5]

Jackson's banking policies would be major issues when it came time to elect the next president. His vice president, Martin Van Buren, was the natural heir to the American throne, but tensions surrounding a rumored banking collapse prevented people from really rallying behind him. Economic historian Peter L. Rousseau tells us that

> by March of 1837 nearly all specified deposits by public receivers were reportedly made in specie. Perhaps surprisingly, land sales, though never again reaching the levels of August 1836, also remained very strong. The Specie Circular reduced but could not eliminate the demand for public lands. Rather, speculation was so intense that it created an extraordinary and somewhat unexpected demand for specie in the West and Southwest. In fact at least $7.3 million in specie was used in U.S. land purchases between July of 1836 and September of 1837, with $1.8 million used in Indiana, $1.4 million in Michigan, and $1.1 million in Illinois.[6]

The boom was unsustainable, and an orchestrated Rothschild-inspired collapse was set to rain down on not only America but England as well. With Jackson's backing, Martin Van Buren easily won the election of 1836 and became the nation's eighth president. When he was elected, the Second Bank had been defeated and the economy was still pretty good. But by the time he took office a full-blown panic was waiting in the wings. Historian William Graham Sumner details how Van Buren got stuck with Jackson's mess.

> Van Buren was now at the height of his ambition; but the financial and commercial storm, which had been gathering for two or three years, the accumulated result of rash ignorance and violent self-will acting on some of the most delicate social interests, was just ready to burst. High prices and high rents had already before the election produced strikes, trades-union conflicts, and labor riots, things which were almost unprecedented in the United States. A bill to annul the specie circular passed the Senate, 41 to 5, and the House, 143 to 59. The President sent it to the State Department at 11:45 P. M.,

March 3, 1837, and filed his reasons for not signing it, it having been sent to him less than ten days before the end of the session.

His reason for not signing the bill was that it was obscure. There was a kind of poetic justice in the fact that Van Buren had to bear the weight of all the consequences of Jackson's acts, which Van Buren had allowed to be committed, because he would not hazard his standing in Jackson's favor by resisting them. Van Buren disliked the reputation of a wire-puller and intriguer, but he had well earned his title the "little magician" by the dexterity with which he had maneuvered himself across the slippery arena of Washington politics and up to the first place. He had just the temper for a politician. Nothing ruffled him. He was thick-skinned, elastic, and tough. He did not win confidence from anybody.

He was, however, a man of more than average ability, and he appears to have been conscious of lowering himself by the political maneuvering which he had practiced. As President he showed the honorable desire to have a statesman-like and high-toned administration, and perhaps to prove that he was more than a creature of Jackson's whim. He could not get a fair chance. The inheritances of party virulence and distrust, which he had taken over from Jackson, were too heavy a weight. He lost his grip on the machine without winning the power of a statesman. He never was able to regain control in the party.[7]

Satirical drawings of the time, such as figure 5.1 (p. 92), addressed this issue. In this particular representation Clay shows the president haunted by the ghost of Commerce, which is seated at the far right end of a table that he shares with a Southern planter (far left) and a New York City Tammany Democrat. Commerce has been strangled by the Specie Circular, which as we know was an extremely unpopular order issued by the Jackson administration in December 1836, requiring collectors of public revenues to accept only gold or silver (i.e., "specie") in payment for public lands. The ghost displays a sheaf of papers, including one marked "Repeal of the Specie Circular," and notices of bank failures in New

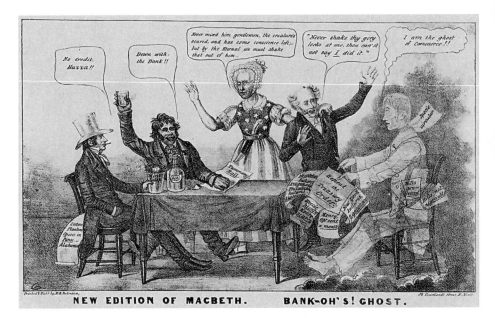

Fig. 5.1. Another satire on the Panic of 1837, again condemning Van Buren's continuation of predecessor Andrew Jackson's hard-money policies as the source of the crisis. *American Political Prints 1766–1876;* HarpWeek.com

Orleans, Philadelphia, and New York. Van Buren recoils at the sight of the specter, exclaiming, "Never shake thy gory locks at me, thou can'st not say *I* did it." Jackson, in a bonnet and dress made of bunting, turns away, saying, "Never mind him, gentlemen, the creature's scared, and has some conscience left; but by the Eternal we must shake that out of him."

By the spring of 1837, Van Buren had succeeded Jackson as president, while a deep national depression loomed as credit lines contracted and loans disappeared. Jackson retreated to his plantation, the Hermitage, down in Tennessee, proclaiming, "I killed the bank!" before he left Washington. Two months after his inauguration President Van Buren met with New York's financial and commercial leaders trying to explain the cause of the crisis. He related it all back to the dangers of central banking, but the money merchants only wanted to hear about a repeal of Jackson's Specie Circular and an eight-month moratorium on bond payments. Van Buren, however, vowed to retain the Treasury order despite being hailed with a ripple of boos from the audience.

Soon bottles were flung, and Van Buren was rushed out of sight, avoiding an angry mob-induced pelting. Within a week the Panic of 1837 erupted when New York banks refused to take payment in specie. On the morning of May 9 more than $652,000 in specie was withdrawn from the vaults of city banks and by that evening, deposits in the bank were less than a thousand dollars. The panic raged on the streets as the public turned on Van Buren, who was now being trashed in the press and blamed for the recent banking crisis. The president found himself in a dire situation given that he lacked the political backing and tools to deal with a nationwide depression without the financial aid of a national bank.

The central banking charter hadn't been reestablished in 1836, and by that Christmas Biddle's bank was closed forever. However, Biddle made good on his promise: a failure to renew his charter ushered in a depression the likes of which had never been seen before; it would wreak havoc on the American economy. Biddle was right—the economy continued to worsen, the real estate market collapsed, and the price of cotton dropped by 20 percent. Banks in both New Orleans and New York City began suspending specie payments, resulting in a panic on Wall Street as specie now became more frequently concentrated in private accounts.

The people panicked too as they hit the streets to protest the sudden economic apocalypse known as the Panic of 1837. Although short, it was America's first great depression. Van Buren received bundles of mail daily, full of letters angrily declaring the unhappiness that Americans felt about the economy. He was under immense pressure to rescind, modify, or scrap Jackson's Treasury order.

Faced with dissenting voices from both sides of the political arena and even from within his own cabinet, Van Buren decided not to do anything that Jackson would not have approved of. And so the panic continued, much as both Jackson and Biddle expected it to do, each knowing the bank war would be a war of attrition. Reginald Charles McGrane explains what happened when limited amounts of specie circulated at that same time as excessive banknotes.

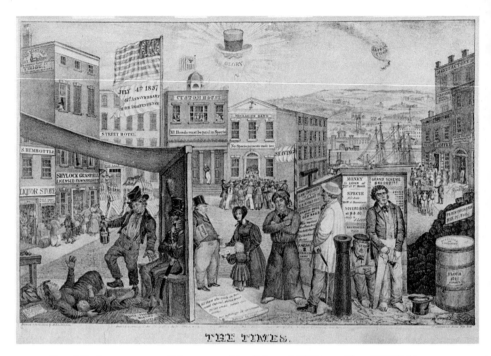

Fig. 5.2. A caricature of the period by Edward Williams Clay (1837) blames Andrew Jackson for hard times.

The suspension of specie payment by the banks was followed by the disappearance of coin as a circulating medium. As specie was at a premium, it was hoarded by those who possessed it, and to carry on necessary business transactions, small bills became the medium of exchange. The New York banks were prohibited from issuing these notes by a law passed in 1835 by the legislature. . . . With the suspension of specie payments, these notes flowed in from the surrounding states until their amount below the denomination of five dollars, was estimated, by 1838, at from three to four million dollars. Problems in Europe, problems of federal government policy, problems with state government policy, and private land speculation created a perfect economic storm.[8]

The Panic of 1837 was a watershed fiscal moment for the U.S. economy as observed by Peter L. Rousseau in the *Journal of Economic History*.

Fig. 5.3. Whig cartoon showing the effects of unemployment on a family that has portraits of Jackson and Van Buren on the wall

The Panic of 1837 was the culmination of a series of policy shifts and unanticipated disturbances that shook the young U.S. economy at the core of its financial structure—the banks of New York City. Over the nine months leading up to the crisis, the specie reserves of these banks came under increasing strain as they reacted to legislation designed to achieve a "political" distribution of the surplus balances among the states and an executive order allegedly aimed at ending speculation in the public lands. With much of the nation's specie diverted from its commercial center, the prospects of shifts in specie demand both domestically and from abroad combined to render the panic inevitable. . . . The crisis highlights several key weaknesses of the antebellum banking system. First, if a branch banking system had been in place, much of the movement of balances associated with the distribution would not have required specie. Second, even if specie had moved South and West, a mechanism for bringing it back to New York would have been in place for use during times of financial stress. Finally, the demise of the Second Bank of the United States at the hands of the Jackson administration left the nation without a lender of last resort to sustain New York's reserves as the public began to lose confidence.[9]

Former president Jackson still blamed the crisis on the Rothschilds, who he suggested would soon be bankrupt. He wrote a letter to Van Buren begging him to hold firm on his Treasury policies and telling him that, despite the fearmongering in the press, the people actually supported them: "The Treasury order is popular with the people everywhere I have passed. But all the speculators and those largely indebted, want more paper, the more it depreciates the easier they can pay their debts. . . . Check the paper mania and the republic is safe and your administration must end in triumph. . . . I say, lay on, temporize not, it is always injurious."[10]

Future president Woodrow Wilson reflected on Van Buren's dilemma in his 1902 book *Critical Changes and Civil War.*

> Within two months after Mr. Van Buren's inauguration General Jackson's "specie circular" had done its work. A sharp financial crisis racked the business of the country from end to end and brought with it a panic stubborn and hopeless, which seemed for months together, as if it had come to stay. It had been strain enough that the money market had had to accommodate itself to the preparations of the Bank of the United States for the winding up of its business, and to the distribution of the surplus among the States. There had been a rapid increase, besides, in the volume of imports since 1832, and considerable sums of specie had had to be sent out of the country to meet the balances of international trade.
>
> The specie circular had come with cruel opportunism. Bankers and borrowers alike had been reckless; credit was already out of breath. When the great sums of paper that had gone west for the purchase of lands from the government came suddenly back by the

Fig. 5.4. The streets of New York during the Panic of 1837
by Edward Williams Clay

hundreds of thousands for redemption there was instant collapse
and panic. Most of the banks had no specie and were utterly unprepared to redeem their notes; those that had specie could afford no
relief—had themselves too little to take care of their own notes.
There was a universal suspension of specie payments, and credit was
dead at a stroke. There had been signs enough of what was about to
happen before the end came. A feverish rise in prices had preceded
it. The price of flour, which had been but five dollars in 1834, had
shot up to eleven dollars per barrel during those first uneasy months
of 1837; the Monday of September he had, it turned out, nothing
to propose except that the interests of the government should be
looked to. The pet banks had gone down with the rest, and it was
necessary that the government should secure its revenues. Mr. Van
Buren had no thought of receding from the policy of the specie
circular; on the contrary, he had himself, amidst the very signs of
acute and increasing distress, issued a similar order with regard to
the transactions of the Post Office. He stood stubborn for specie
payments, banks or no banks, and had aggressive spokesmen at his

back in Congress: notably Mr. [Silas] Wright and Mr. Benton in the Senate.

The President and his spokesmen had nothing to propose for the relief of business. He believed, as Mr. Calhoun did, that palliatives would only prolong the unavoidable misery of readjustment and the return to sound methods of business, the substitution of real for fictitious values and of production for speculation, and that, bad as they were, things would right themselves more quickly and more wholesomely without the intervention of legislation than by means of it. His plan was, to cut once for all the connection of the government with the banks, and provide for the custody, handling, and disbursement of the revenues by the Treasury alone. For three years, through two Congresses, he fought doggedly for his purpose and won at last in midsummer, 1840. Then he got exactly what he wanted. An "Independent Treasury Act," signed July 4, 1840, provided that the Treasury of the United States should itself supply vaults and places of deposit for the revenues at Washington and at other cities appointed for their receipt; that all federal officers charged with their receipt, safe keeping, or disbursement should be put under proper and sufficient bonds for their careful and honest use and custody; and that all payments thereafter made either to or by the United States should be made in gold or silver only.

It had not been possible to bring the first Congress of Mr. Van Buren's term to accept this scheme. Twice adopted by the Senate, now at last Democratic, it had been twice rejected by the House, where a section of the Democratic majority united with the Whigs to defeat it. Meanwhile the President had been obliged to do without law what he wished Congress to authorize by law. The banks of deposit had suspended payment; there was nothing to be done but to direct the agents of the Treasury to keep and account for as best they could the moneys that came into their hands. Meanwhile, too, the country went staggering and bewildered through its season of bitter ruin. There had been nothing like it before in all the history of business in America. Utter collapse and despair came, soon or late, upon every sort of undertaking the year through.[11]

In 1838, Congress eventually repealed Jackson's Specie Circular, and Van Buren, who was pressured into going along, reluctantly bowed to its wishes. But this backing down only led to another serious economic catastrophe—the Panic of 1839—which continued the tough times. Repercussions of the panic extended throughout the economy as businesses either cut back production or folded. Workers lost their jobs in record numbers when shoe and textile factories laid off thousands of employees. Banks closed. Unemployment soared. In New York City a five-dollar hike in the price of flour sparked a riot in Greenwich Village, resulting in looting and chaos that had to be stamped out by the militia. By 1840 the American banking system had crumbled under the relenting pressure from British (Rothschild) creditors, and eventually almost every bank failed, especially those dependent on the cotton trade. These panics engulfed every class of citizen and shook up all phases of American life for seven long years. But Andrew Jackson felt no remorse for the panics or for anything else he had done while in the Oval Office.

The approbation I have received from the people everywhere on my return home on the close of my official life has been a source of much gratification to me. I have been met at every point by numerous Democrat-Republican friends and many repenting Whigs, with a hearty welcome and expressions of "well done thou faithful servant." This is truly the patriot's reward, the summit of my gratification, and will be my solace to my grace. When I review the arduous administration through which I have passed, the formidable opposition, to its very close, of the combined talents, wealth and power of the whole aristocracy of the United States, aided as it is, by the monied monopolies of the whole country, with their corrupting influence, with which we had to contend, I am truly thankful to my

God for this happy result. It displays the virtue and power of the sovereign people, and that all must bow to their will. But it was the voice of this sovereign will that so nobly sustained us against this formidable power and enabled me to pass through my administration so as to meet its approbation.[12]

Jackson's popularity waned after his retirement as most Americans blamed him for the depression. But Jackson knew that he had killed the banks and succeeded in throwing out the Rothschilds' central banking scheme altogether—an incredible achievement that lasted for seventy-seven years. He didn't care whether the ordinary American understood what he had done; he simply told them that their grandchildren would thank him. Jackson had put his archrival Nicholas Biddle out of business as well.

Like others before him, life after the bank war wasn't kind to Biddle, who was so reviled that mobs stalked him weekly in Philadelphia, forcing him to hire armed security and bar the doors and windows of his home. Although the Second Bank had been destroyed by Jackson, Biddle created a new bank called the U.S. Bank of Pennsylvania, a private commercial bank that he ran under a state charter. But in private banking and without the help of the Rothschilds, Biddle could not replicate the success he had enjoyed as a central banker. He also made the mistake of cornering the cotton market with his own bank-issued funds. This scam, which he could do easily at a central bank, wound up leaving him broke and indicted for fraud. Yes . . . the charges were eventually dismissed, but creditors now avoided Biddle like the plague, and his U.S. Bank of Pennsylvania went belly up a few years after the Panic of 1839.

The collapse of the bank, an array of civil suits, and constant harassment by the government eventually consumed what was left of Biddle's once vast personal fortune. With a ruined reputation and empty pockets Biddle retreated to his wife's estate north of Philadelphia. On the banks of the Delaware River this Adalusia village estate featuring fabulous Greek Revival architecture is where Biddle spent his final days:

dying from depression, heartbreak, and other unspecified maladies at the age of fifty-eight, Biddle's fall from banking grace brought a huge smile to the face of Andrew Jackson, who outlived him by a year.

Jackson died on his Hermitage plantation in Nashville in the summer of 1845, at age seventy-eight, from chronic tuberculosis, terminal dropsy, and heart failure. He was buried next to his beloved Rachel on the Hermitage's grounds. During the general's funeral, which was packed full of admirers, Jackson's pet parrot was kicked out of the service for swearing like a sailor. Although a war hero and a celebrated American in his own time, Jackson's legacy has been largely eclipsed. Mere vestiges of this legacy are more or less limited to his image on America's twenty-dollar bill and his portrayal in the nation's history books as a murderer of Native Americans, if he's even remembered at all.

The fact that he was chosen to be on the twenty-dollar bill has always been a mystery. Was this a silent nod of respect by the Rothschilds? After all, to this day Andrew Jackson has been the only president to defeat them. If it was a sign of respect, that respect seems to now have run its course with the recent news that he will be replaced on the twenty-dollar bill by a woman. The Senate proponents of this measure happen to be Democrats, who are probably oblivious to the fact that their political party was created by Jackson in the first place.

With the death of "Old Hickory" and a great depression coming to a slow end, the 1840s were marching toward a new decade after a long rebuilding process. People were still poor, jobs were sparse, and the great unknown to the west was still dangerous territory. The Rothschilds had been defeated but still controlled most of Europe and were patiently biding their time while formulating plots and strategizing about how to conquer America. Imagine their luck when they discovered how to get Americans to fight each other to the death while they kicked back and watched. As the dawn of the Civil War loomed, Jackson's idea of "Manifest Destiny" and westward expansion became a reality as pioneers, farmers, and settlers left home only to find more head-scratching discoveries relating to mysterious mounds, lost cultures, and ancient giants when they did so.

6

Ancient Giants and Westward Expansion

1847–1857

A Gleam of Sunshine

But now, alas! the place seems changed
Thou art no longer here
Part of the sunshine of the scene
With thee did disappear
Though thoughts, deep-rooted in my heart
Like pine-trees dark and high
Subdue the light of noon, and breathe
A low and ceaseless sigh
This memory brightens o'er the past
As when the sun, concealed
Behind some cloud that near us hangs
Shines on a distant field

HENRY WADSWORTH LONGFELLOW

It is the mark of a great man that he puts to flight all ordinary calculations. He is at once sublime and touching, childlike and of the race of giants.

HONORÉ DE BALZAC

As the frontier lands west of the Allegheny Mountains were settled, curiosities consisting of giant bones continued to confound their discoverers. Spanish missionaries as far west as California were discovering twelve-foot-tall skeletons but were forced by the Natives to rebury them. In Ohio alone there were rumored to be more than ten thousand mounds dotting the landscape, with more than half of these mounds presumed to house the remains of ancient giants. In 1839 the Miamisburg Mound, one of the biggest mounds in Ohio, had been excavated by Dr. John Treon. His hired hands dug up a few giant bones ten feet beneath the surface. The bones were preserved by Dr. Treon, who claimed that one jawbone found in the mound could easily slip over the chin of the world's tallest man. More than sixty years later another mound within the Miamisburg area revealed more giant surprises. *The Middletown Signal* reports:

> The skeleton of a giant found near Miamisburg is the cause of much discussion not only among the curious and illiterate but among the learned scientists of the world. The body of a man more gigantic than any ever recorded in human history, has been found in the Miami Valley, in Ohio. The skeleton it is calculated must have belonged to a man 8 feet 1 and ½ inches in height. It was found within a half mile of Miamisburg in a locality which contains many relics of the mound builders. Edward Gobhart and Edward Kauffman discovered it while they were working in a gravel pit. Kauffman struck a hard substance with his pick and examining it found it to be a skull. When they unearthed the whole skeleton and realized its size they were aghast. The skeleton is of prehistoric age, being fossilized, its giant proportions present a puzzling problem to the archaeologist.
>
> The bones have been placed on exhibition and many are the curious sight seers who have passed in wonder before them. It is claimed by residents of the Miami Valley that a prehistoric race once inhabited the region and erected the largest mound in the country.[1]

Fig. 6.1. The great mound at Miamisburg, Ohio, *Western Gazatteer* (1847)

The details pertaining to this discovery were examined by multiple scientists, including the Smithsonian's head of anthropology. Intent on whitewashing all mention of giants from the public record, he continued to insist that giants didn't exist and claimed that the unearthed bones were those of ancient animals. These scientists admitted to having evidence of only one unusually large skeleton, which they said was a Native American who must have suffered from pituitary gigantism. That's all the Smithsonian admitted to, dismissing a vast number of reports from the 1800s that indicated otherwise. Sure a lot of those reports were hoaxes, but most of them were sincere in telling it like it was in a world still free of the religious dogma presented by the theory of evolution. In 1839, near Pascagoula Bay in Jackson County, Mississippi, an ancient fortification built entirely of seashells had been discovered. Below the ruins of this fort were charred coals, strange bits of broken pottery, and a grave of human bodies, some of which were giants with tremendous skulls.

A giant discovered in Nashville hit the front pages nationwide in 1845.

We are informed on the most reliable authority that a person in Franklin County, Tennessee, while digging a well, a few weeks since, found a human skeleton, at the depth of fifty feet, which measures eighteen feet in length. The immense frame was entire with an unimportant exception in one of the extremities. It has been visited by several of the principal members of the medical faculty in Nashville, and pronounced unequivocally, by all, the skeleton of a huge man. The bone of the thigh measured five feet; and it was computed that the height of the living man, making the proper allowance for muscles, must have been at least twenty feet. The finder had been offered eight thousand dollars for it, but had determined not to sell it at any price until first exhibiting it for twelve months. . . . History informs us that the Emperor Maximum was 8 feet 6 inches in height. In the reign of Claudius a man was brought from Arabia 9 feet 9 inches tall. John Middleton, of Lancashire, England, was 9 feet 3 inches, and Cotter, the Irish Giant, 8 feet 7 inches. But our American skeleton, if we have really found such a one, will throw all other Giants in the shade.[2]

The *Western Review Weekly* from Franklin, Tennessee, adds:

There have been recently dug up in Williamson County, Tennessee, seven miles from Franklin, the bones of a giant and no mistake. We have conversed with an intelligent and enterprising gentleman of our city, who has seen, examined, and purchased an interest in the skeleton. From him we derive the following facts: A Mr. Shumate was boring for water near his residence, upon a hill of considerable extent and eminence, situated in a rocky, mountainous section of country, where the bones were discovered about 60 feet beneath the surface. They were immediately exhumed, and were found embedded in a strata of the hardest kind of clay which had apparently filled an extensive cavern or opening in the rock. The position of the skeleton was that of a recumbent, making an angle of the horizon. The bones are not at all petrified as in the case with most of the skeleton monsters of animals which have been discovered in our country, but are, nevertheless, in a most perfect state of preservation, and weigh in the aggregate about 1500 pounds! No doubt rests in the minds of any who have seen or examined them that these bones belong to the genus homo.

All the larger and characteristic bones are entire, and the skull, arms and thigh bones, knee pans, shoulder sockets and collar bones remove all skepticism as to their humanity. The whole skeleton, we are informed, is about 18 feet high, and must have stood a full 19 feet "in his stockings" (if he wore any). The bones of the thigh and leg measure 6 feet 6 inches, so that our friend, "the General," could have marched erect, in full military costume, between the giant's legs. The skull is described as being about 2–3 times the size of a flour barrel, and capable of holding in its cavities near two bushels; a coffee cup of good size could be put into the eye sockets—and the jaw teeth, which are all perfect even to the enamel, would weigh from 3½ to 6 pounds, some of the smaller ones which were loose have been weighed—the front teeth are missing. These teeth bear the evidence of extreme age, from their cavities are apparent diminution from use in wearing away. An eminent physician and anatomist, properly assisted, is engaged in having the skeleton put together and the small deficiencies supplied by art.

We are further informed by our fellow citizen, who has purchased an interest of one fourth in this interesting and wonderful curiosity, that it will be ready for exhibition in about one month's time, when it will start on its tour thro' the civilized world, and proceeding from New Orleans will shortly be among us here. Our fellow townsman keeps the price he paid for his interest a secret, but says that $50,000 has been offered and refused for the whole of this curiosity.[3]

Even the *New York Herald* got in on the act, albeit reporting in a tone less feverish.

The skeleton discovered in Williamson County in this State, and supposed to be that of a human being, has frequently been referred to, within a few days past, in the House of Representatives. . . . This skeleton was found about sixty feet beneath the surface of the earth, embedded in a stratum of the hardest kind of clay. The bones are said to be in a perfect state of preservation. . . . This gentleman, when he walked the earth, was about eighteen feet high, and when clothed in flesh must have weighed not less than 3000 pounds. The bones of the thigh and leg measure six feet six inches; his skull is said to be about two-thirds the size of a flour barrel, and capable of holding in its cavities near two bushels. A coffee cup of good size could be put in the eye-sockets.[4]

Unfortunately the giant eighteen-foot skeleton dug up in Tennessee proved to be nothing more than the flawed skeleton of a young mastodon. However, the veracity of this was not determined until after it had been assembled with makeshift human bones that were tied together, forming a standing giant display that was exhibited throughout the Mississippi Valley. It eventually made its way to New Orleans, where Professor William Marbury Carpenter of the Louisiana Medical College pronounced it neither man nor merman but mastodon. This ended the hoax of the Tennessee giant and disappointed museum goers in New Orleans.

Regardless, in the Ohio Valley ancient graveyards were being excavated all over the place. As mounds were destroyed to make way for the settling of new lands, more skeletons came to light. Some of them were of giants, some were of normal size, and some were clearly those of children and frightened mothers. It seems as if an ancient and violent battle had once raged throughout the Ohio Valley. Was this the battleground of America's first civil war?

Predating the American Civil War by thousands of years, the ancient mound-building culture that disappeared into the abyss has mystified scholars and antiquarians for centuries. Apart from the bones discovered, archaeological records hold almost no data from this time period, leaving us dependent on Native American oral mythologies. However, the traditions of these Natives speak of a time before their own when a race of giants once ruled the Ohio Valley. These same giants eventually wiped each other out but not before leaving behind a plethora of mysterious mounds as testaments to their ancient legacy. This ancient legacy has been removed from the official annals of American history, only to be uncovered by curious individuals intent on ascertaining the truth about America's past.

Similar archaic mounds have also been found in the South and include Louisiana's Watson Brake and Poverty Point mounds, South Carolina's Fig Island mounds, and the Sapelo mound complex of Georgia. Mounds have also been discovered in Oregon, where an ancient race long forgotten by the local Natives was excavated, revealing giant bones and elongated skulls. The identity of the mound builders was a mystery back then, and it remains a mystery to this day.

As giant skeletons continued to be dug up and exposed most eventually disappeared into private hands or got lost altogether in the halls of academia. But as the 1840s drew to a close, America's curiosity with

Fig. 6.2. Louisiana State University campus mounds, by Spatms

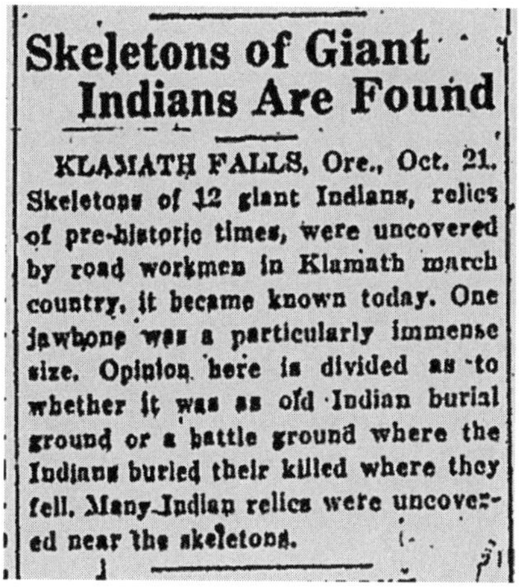

Skeletons of Giant Indians Are Found

KLAMATH FALLS, Ore., Oct. 21. Skeletons of 12 giant Indians, relics of pre-historic times, were uncovered by road workmen in Klamath march country, it became known today. One jawbone was a particularly immense size. Opinion here is divided as to whether it was an old Indian burial ground or a battle ground where the Indians buried their killed where they fell. Many Indian relics were uncovered near the skeletons.

Fig. 6.3. Newspaper article of the time about giants being discovered in Oregon. tnephilim.blogspot.com

them continued unabated, especially when reports of them continued to be covered and sensationalized by the press.

One man who had been bitten by the "giant bug" was a curious and forward-thinking lawyer, congressman, member of the Illinois state legislature, and peace activist (who voted against going to war with Mexico): Abraham Lincoln. At six feet four inches tall, Lincoln was already a giant when compared with the average man of his day. As such, he'd had a Victorian bed custom-built to accommodate his lanky frame. Lincoln joked that the ancient giants who once roamed the Midwest must have been his ancestors. He had been raised in mound country and had been schooled on the subject early on. Later his interest in the mound builders and their long-lost culture would find him traveling by steamboat up the Ohio River to investigate stories about them firsthand.

In addition to being fascinated with the ancient mounds, Lincoln was obsessed with natural history, archaeology, and the ideas of lost cultures and Atlantis. He fantasized about having a career as a natural history professor but, by his own admission, had been guided by higher powers to a career in law and politics. Lincoln's notebooks were full of writings about animals, nature, mysticism, and Native American mythology. In an unpublished essay about natural history, which he wrote in 1848 while bored one day in Congress, he made a curious reference to the mounds and giants: "The eyes of that extinct species of

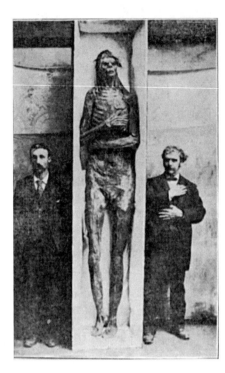

Fig. 6.4. A giant mound builder on display. tnephilim .blogspot.com

giant, whose bones fill the mounds of America, have gazed on Niagara as our eyes do now."*5

Lincoln was preceded in his fascination with the mounds of Ohio by America's first president, George Washington, then a young man and still a British citizen working for the Ohio Company, planting survey markers throughout the epicenter of mound-builder country. Washington was impressed by the mounds between the valleys of the Muskingum and the Miami and was intent on building a Masonic lodge near the massive mound complex in Marietta, but his involvement in the Revolutionary War precluded him from doing so. Thomas Jefferson, "the father of American archaeology," excavated a mound near his home in Monticello around 1780 but didn't report finding any giant bones. Masonic poets Ralph Waldo Emerson and Henry Wadsworth Longfellow were also mound enthusiasts, ranking the Ohio mounds right up there with Stonehenge and the Egyptian pyramids.

---

*http://quod.lib.umich.edu/l/lincoln/lincoln2/1:6?rgn=div1;view=fulltext

Fig. 6.5. Giants of Santa Rosa Island: a cemetery containing abalone shells
radiocarbon dated at 7,070 years. Tops of skulls painted red.
Several skeletons measured over seven feet tall.
Photo courtesy of Santa Barbara Museum of Natural History

Georgia's Sand-Dunes Yield Startling
Proof of a Prehistoric Race of Giants

The Archaeologists Were
Mystified at
Finding
Skeletons
of Men
Who Were
7 Feet
Tall

Fig. 6.6. Giants found along the coast of Georgia.
The Portsmouth Times, 1936; tnephilim.blogspot.com

Despite the interest that prominent Americans showed in the mounds and their curious contents, these discoveries were such anomalies that they continued to be marginalized. Archaeologist Ephraim George Squier and physician Edwin Davis spent two years traveling, surveying, and interviewing people whose land featured mounds for their book *Ancient Monuments of the Mississippi Valley*. This was the first book that the newly formed Smithsonian Institution published, and free copies of it were distributed to members of Congress.

Lincoln read a copy, yawned, and penned his rebuttal. Lincoln was miffed that only two usages of the word "giant" appeared in the book. The first was a mention of "giant temples" in Georgia, and the second described a "giant" man-shaped effigy mound in Wisconsin. To nobody's surprise and certainly not Lincoln's, not one single mention of any giant skeletons were reported anywhere in Squier and Davis's Smithsonian-approved book.

Lincoln was an eclectic man who had an odd mixture of friends. He could just as easily dine with a stuffy, conservative intellectual as he could with a roomful of naturalists, Native shamans, and armchair mystics. He was also keen to hang out with Rosicrucians and Freemasons. He may have shared his interest in giants, lost cultures, and other occult philosophies with two Masons: his father-in-law, Robert Smith Todd, as well as his former foe yet fellow mound enthusiast Henry Clay.

Lincoln's wife was the daughter of Clay's friend Robert Smith Todd. Todd was a wealthy banker who funded the research of two heralded professors, John D. Clifford and Constantine Rafinesque, who also catalogued the findings of the mounds of Kentucky and Ohio. Clay was extremely influential in Ohio, a state whose pioneering cities of Marietta, Cincinnati, Portsmouth, Chillicothe, and Worthington all had initially been founded as Masonic towns. Clay was the former grand master and grand orator of the Grand Lodge of Kentucky; at the same time he was also a senator of Kentucky. Clay founded the Whig Party in opposition to Jackson's Democrats, and as soon as the Jacksonian era ended the Whigs became the prime presidential force in the White House.

Clay had been able to help get fellow Ohio Valley Freemason William Henry Harrison elected president in 1841, but the elderly Harrison died after only a year in office, leaving the job to his vice president and fellow Mason, John Tyler. Tyler remained president until being replaced by another Mason, James K. Polk, who was succeeded by another Mason, Zachary Taylor, who was succeeded by a member of the Anti-Masonic Party (who was still a Mason), Millard Fillmore. Succeeding Fillmore was the "no doubt about it" Mason, Franklin Pierce, who happens to also be one of the worst presidents ever, according to most mainstream polls. The super Mason James Buchanan succeeded Pierce and left the gates to the Civil War wide open by the time that his successor, Abraham Lincoln, was ready to take his place as president. Lincoln had never formally joined a Masonic lodge. He had, however, flirted with the idea, but for some reason withdrew his application before starting his presidential campaign.

The presidency had been a long time coming for Lincoln given that he had participated behind the scenes in presidential campaigns and the political process since joining Congress in 1848. Nearly a decade later Lincoln was gearing up for his run for the presidency.

As the years that led up to the Civil War intensified with threats of secession and violence, settlers moving west continued to unearth giant skeletons and odd ancient artifacts. And when white settlers first arrived in western New York the area was littered with the works of an earlier people. Stone walls and roads, earthen mounds, and ancient fortifications were prevalent, but the Native Americans of New York provided little information about the people who had left them there. The mysterious mound-building culture became a victim of the plow, and after a time only a relatively few number of mounds were left to reveal their ancient curiosities.

In *Illustrations of the Ancient Monuments of Western New York* the author describes a mound in Cattaraugus County's Conewango Valley that once housed eight giant skeletons. But all of the ancient bones except for a twenty-eight-inch-high bone crumbled when exposed to the Conewango Valley air. More giants were discovered nearby: An old mound near Cassadaga Lake produced a nearly nine-foot-tall goliath, and settlers removing a tree stump in the town of Carrollton were shocked to find a graveyard full of giants beneath the stump's roots. In Buffalo two bizarre giant skulls with "portentous, protruding lower jaw and canine forehead"[6] were discovered alongside strange pottery shards and arranged in a manner completely foreign to common ancient burial grounds. In 1855 workmen digging a cellar in Concord, New Hampshire, discovered a giant with double rows of teeth. This giant ended up being displayed and preserved locally in Dr. William Prescott's cabinet before disappearing after being loaned to Yale.

In 1856 the *New York Times* reported on a giant discovery made in Wheeling, West Virginia.

A day or two since, some workmen engaged in subsoiling the grounds of Sheriff WICKHAN, at his vineyard in East Wheeling, came across a human skeleton. Although much decayed, there was little difficulty in identifying it, by placing the bones, which could not have belonged to others than a human body, in their original position. The impression made by the skeleton in the earth, and the skeleton itself, were measured by the Sheriff and a brother in the craft locale, both of whom were prepared to swear that it was *ten feet nine inches in length*. Its jaws and teeth were almost as large as those of a horse. The bones are to be seen at the sheriff's office.[7]

Apparently there was no further word on what had happened to the sheriff's giant bones. A year later the *Boston Medical Journal* reprinted a story found in the Burlington, Iowa, *State Gazette* that read:

While some workmen were engaged in excavating for the cellar of Governor Grimes's new building, on the corner of Maine and Valley streets, they came upon an arched vault some ten feet square, which, on being opened, was found to contain eight human skeletons of gigantic proportions. The walls of the vault were about fourteen inches thick, well laid up with cement or indestructible mortar. The vault is about six feet deep from the base to the arch. The skeletons are in a good state of preservation, and we venture to say are the largest human remains ever found, being a little over eight feet long.[8]

As 1860 approached and the discovery of ancient giants began to fly in the face of Darwin's theory of evolution and the archaeology principles being established by the Smithsonian, the suppression of their existence and the battle to rewrite America's past began to take hold. Another battle was brewing in America as the Civil War and all its complex intricacies were boiling to the point of running over. Mixing behind the scenes to make this war happen were the usual list of nefarious characters, including the Rothschilds, who were hell-bent on making America pay for not rechartering their central bank. They had many tricks up their sleeves to ensure the bank was rechartered.

One of their secret weapons was rumored to be Abraham Lincoln himself, a man some researchers claim was more than a Rothschild agent—he was actually a member of the Rothschild bloodline who had been secretly placed in a position of power. Did some of Lincoln's genetic makeup come from that elite Rothschild lineage? Did the Rothschilds really have a hand in launching the Civil War? As 1860 dawned, both Lincoln and the Rothschilds looked toward the upcoming election with the assurance that life in America would soon be changed forever.

7

The Rothschilds and the Civil War

1858–1861

I am a soldier and my speech is rough and plain
I'm not much used to writing and I hate to give you pain
But I promised I would do it and he thought it might be so
If it came from one who loved him perhaps it would ease the
* blow*
By this time you must have guessed the truth I fain will hide
And you'll pardon me for rough soldier words while I tell you
* how he died*
It was in the mortal battle, it rained the shot and shell
I was standing close beside him and I saw him when he fell
So I took him in my arms and laid him on the grass
It was going against orders but they thought to let it pass
'Twas a minie ball that struck him, it entered at his side
But we didn't think it fatal till this morning when he died
"Last night I wanted so to live, I seemed so young to go.
This week I passed my birthday. I was just nineteen, you
* know.*
When I thought of all I planned to do it seemed so hard to
* die*

But now I pray to God for grace and all my cares gone by."
And here his voice grew weaker as he partly raised his head
And whispered "Goodbye, mother," and your soldier boy was
dead
I carved another headboard as skillful as I could
And if you wish to find it I can tell you where it stood
I send you back his hymn book and the cap he used to wear
The lock I cut the night before of his bright, curly hair
I send you back his Bible. The night before he died
I turned its leaves together and read it by his side
I'll keep the belt he was wearing, he told me so to do
It had a hole upon the side just where the ball went through

AUTHOR UNKNOWN, WRITTEN
DURING THE CIVIL WAR

I have too great a soul to die like a criminal.

JOHN WILKES BOOTH

The events leading up to the Civil War were replete with international intrigue and Southern skullduggery. Mainstream historians usually only focus on states' rights and the issue of slavery as the leading cause of the conflict, excluding the external threats posed by the Rothschilds and the Bank of England. Still bitter from their defeat in the War of 1812 and for losing out against Jackson in the bank war, which saw the defeat of their central banking scheme, the Rothschilds had been planning to conquer America since those losses, or at least divide and conquer it. Using their agents to rally the people against slavery led to tighter legal restrictions and embargos on the South.

The South, of course, responded with secession and vowed to fight to the death to preserve their racist way of life. These tensions between North and South put the Rothschilds on notice given that they had maintained close business ties with the South's cotton-growing aristocracy. These Southern plantation owners benefited greatly from the banking institutions and cotton manufacturers in England. In fact, by the time the war was set to break out the South was swarming with British agents working on behalf of the Rothschilds. They were positive that the Southern slavery issue was America's Achilles' heel and once sliced open would provide the back door through which they could sneak in and begin their assault. Theirs was a brilliant plan to divide America on the issue of slavery and pit brother against brother as the Southern slave states dueled it out with the Northern industrial states. The problem was that slavery was widespread everywhere in America. In both the North and the South if you were rich there was a good chance that you owned slaves.

THE CENSUS CHART FOR 1860	
Free colored persons	476,748
Total free population	27,233,198
Total number of slaves	3,950,528
Slaves as percentage of the population	13 percent
Total number of families	5,155,608
Total number of slaveholders	393,975
Percentage of families owning slaves	8 percent

The total percentage of slaves for the two combined regions that made up the Northern and the Southern states was 30.8 percent. A breakdown of the percentage of people who were slaves in each individual state is as follows:

Mississippi: 49 percent
South Carolina: 46 percent
Georgia: 37 percent
Alabama: 35 percent
Florida: 34 percent

Louisiana: 29 percent

Texas: 28 percent

North Carolina: 28 percent

Virginia: 26 percent

Tennessee: 25 percent

Kentucky: 23 percent

Arkansas: 20 percent

Missouri: 13 percent

Maryland: 12 percent

Delaware: 3 percent

Although the North had a large number of abolitionists and pro-gressives, they also had racist laws and violent lynch mobs. As explained on the PBS show *Africans in America,*

> to the fugitive slave fleeing a life of bondage, the North was a land of freedom. Or so he or she thought. Upon arriving there, the fugitive found that, though they were no longer slaves, neither were they free. African Americans in the North lived in a strange state of semi-freedom. The North may have emancipated its slaves, but it was not ready to treat the blacks as citizens . . . or sometimes even as human beings. Northern racism grew directly out of slavery and the ideas used to justify the institution. The concepts of "black" and "white" did not arrive with the first Europeans and Africans, but grew on American soil.
>
> During Andrew Jackson's administration, racist ideas took on new meaning. Jackson brought in the "Age of the Common Man." Under his administration, working-class people gained rights they had not before possessed, particularly the right to vote. But the only people who benefited were white men. Blacks, Native Americans, and women were not included. This was a time when European immigrants were pouring into the North. Many of these people had faced discrimination and hardship in their native countries. But

in America they found their rights expanding rapidly. They had entered a country in which they were part of a privileged category called "white." Classism and ethnic prejudices did exist among white Americans and had a tremendous impact on people's lives. But the bottom line was that for white people in America, no matter how poor or degraded they were, they knew there was a class of people below them. Poor whites were considered superior to blacks, and to natives as well, simply by virtue of being white. Because of this, most identified with the rest of the white race and defended the institution of slavery. Working-class whites did this even though slavery did not benefit them directly and was in many ways against their best interests.

Before 1800, free African-American men had nominal rights of citizenship. In some places they could vote, serve on juries, and work in skilled trades. But as the need to justify slavery grew stronger, and racism started solidifying, free blacks gradually lost the rights that they did have. Through intimidation, changing laws, and mob violence, whites claimed racial supremacy, and increasingly denied blacks their citizenship. And in 1857 the Dred Scott decision formally declared that blacks were not citizens of the United States.

In the northeastern states, blacks faced discrimination in many forms. Segregation was rampant, especially in Philadelphia, where blacks were excluded from concert halls, public transportation, schools, churches, orphanages, and other places. They were also forced out of the skilled professions in which they had been working. And soon after the turn of the century, black men began to lose the right to vote—a right that many states had granted following the Revolutionary War. Simultaneously, voting rights were being expanded for whites. New Jersey took the black vote away in 1807; in 1818 Connecticut took it away from black men who had not voted previously; in 1821 New York took away property requirements for white men to vote, but kept them for blacks. This meant that only a tiny percentage of black men could vote in that state.

In 1838, Pennsylvania took the vote away entirely. The only states in which black men never lost the right to vote were Maine, New Hampshire, Vermont, and Massachusetts.

The situation in what was then the northwest region of the country was even worse. In Ohio, the state constitution of 1802 deprived blacks of the right to vote, to hold public office, and to testify against whites in court. Over the next five years, more restrictions were placed on blacks. They could not live in Ohio without a certificate proving their free status; they had to post a $500 bond "to pay for their support in case of want," and they were prohibited from joining the state militia. In 1831 blacks were excluded from serving on juries and were not allowed admittance to state poorhouses, insane asylums, and other institutions.

Fortunately, some of these laws were not stringently enforced, or it would have been virtually impossible for any black to immigrate to Ohio. In Illinois there were severe restrictions on free blacks entering the state, and Indiana barred them altogether. Michigan, Iowa, and Wisconsin were no friendlier. Because of this, the black populations of the northwestern states never exceeded 1 percent. Blacks also faced violence at the hands of white northerners. Individual cases of assault and murder occurred throughout the North, as did daily insults and harassment. Between 1820 and 1850, northern blacks also became the frequent targets of mob violence. Whites looted, tore down, and burned black homes, churches, schools, and meeting halls. They stoned, beat, and sometimes murdered blacks. Philadelphia was the site of the worst and most frequent mob violence.[1]

In 1703 slavery in the North had been a common thing. Indeed, 42 percent of New York City's households had slaves. By 1775 in New York City more than 3,000 slaves accounted for 30 to 40 percent of the city's workforce. Nowadays institutional slavery makes up a good chunk of the workforce as more than 10,000 people alone are working for 15 cents an hour at the notorious prison on Riker's Island. For-profit prisons have kept slavery alive while simultaneously ensuring that the minimum wage (paid to prisoners, i.e., slaves) remains low as businesses struggle to compete with the 15-cent-an-hour prison workforce.

More than 2.2 million people are currently incarcerated in jails and prisons in the United States, a population that has increased more than 500 percent over the past forty years. Presently America accounts for about 5 percent of the world's population; yet in terms of the world's prison population we house more than 25 percent of our populace! Rwanda, a third-world country, is a distant second place, with a measly 5 percent of its citizens locked up. Of course, the increase in imprisonment in America has been mostly for drug possession, which is a direct attack on young men of color. Nearly half of the 2.2 million U.S. prisoners are black males. Put another way, about 1 in 9 black American males between the ages of 18 and 35 are now in prison, more than 1 million are on probation, and if current trends continue one-third of all black men will at some point wind up in prison in their lifetime. Sadly, there are more black men in prison, on probation, or on parole than were enslaved in 1860.

Slavery existed in every American colony until Vermont became the first state to eradicate it in 1777. Emancipation wasn't complete in New York until 1827. The Spanish and Portuguese exported more than a million slaves from Africa to the New World long before the first handful ever reached Virginia. Scholars estimate that nearly ten million Africans were forced into slavery and shipped to the Americas. Every Western New World colony was basically a slave colony. French Canada, Jamaica, Pennsylvania, Virginia, Cuba, and Brazil all got their economic start thanks to slavery. The following excerpt from SlaveNorth.com explains further.

> Slavery was still very much alive, and in some places even expanding,
> in the northern colonies of British North America in the generation
> before the American Revolution. The spirit of liberty in 1776 and

the rhetoric of rebellion against tyranny made many Americans conscious of the hypocrisy of claiming natural human rights for themselves, while at the same time denying them to Africans. Nonetheless, most of the newly free states managed to postpone dealing with the issue of slavery, citing the emergency of the war with Britain. That war, however, proved to be the real liberator of the northern slaves. Wherever it marched, the British army gave freedom to any slave who escaped within its lines. This was sound military policy: it disrupted the economic system that was sustaining the Revolution. Since the North saw much longer and more extensive incursions by British troops, its slave population drained away at a higher rate than the South's. At the same time, the governments in northern American states began to offer financial incentives to slave owners who freed their black men, if the emancipated slaves then served in the state regiments fighting the British.

When the Northern states gave up the last remnants of legal slavery, in the generation after the Revolution, their motives were a mix of piety, morality, and ethics; fear of a growing black population; practical economics; and the fact that the Revolutionary War had broken the Northern slave owners' power and drained off much of the slave population. An exception was New Jersey, where the slave population actually increased during the [Revolutionary] war. Slavery lingered there until the Civil War, with the state reporting 236 slaves in 1850 and 18 as late as 1860. The business of emancipation in the North amounted to the simple matters of 1) determining how to compensate slave owners for the few slaves they had left, and 2) making sure newly freed slaves would be marginalized economically and politically in their home communities, and that nothing in the state's constitution would encourage fugitive slaves from elsewhere to settle there. But in the generally conservative, local process of emancipating a small number of northern slaves, the northern leadership turned its back on slavery as a national problem.[2]

Slavery wasn't just something that whites indulged in. Free blacks owned slaves as early as 1654 and continued doing so right through the Civil War. In fact the very first slave owner in American history, according to colonial records, was a free black man named Anthony Johnson.

Prior to 1655 there were no legal slaves in the colonies, only indentured servants. All masters were required to free their servants after their time was up. Seven years was the limit that an indentured servant could be held. Upon their release they were granted 50 acres of land. This included any Negro purchased from slave traders. Negroes were also granted 50 acres upon their release. Anthony Johnson was a Negro from modern-day Angola. He was brought to the US to work on a tobacco farm in 1619. In 1622 he was almost killed when Powhatan Indians attacked the farm. 52 out of 57 people on the farm perished in the attack. He married a female black servant while working on the farm. When Anthony was released he was legally recognized as a "free Negro" and ran a successful farm. In 1651 he held 250 acres and five black indentured servants. In 1654, it was time for Anthony to release John Casor, a black indentured servant. Instead Anthony told Casor he was extending his time. Casor left and became employed by the free white man Robert Parker. Anthony Johnson sued Robert Parker in the Northampton Court in 1654. In 1655, the court ruled that Anthony Johnson could hold John Casor indefinitely. The court gave judicial sanction for blacks to own slave of their own race. Thus Casor became the first permanent slave and Johnson the first slave owner. Whites still could not legally hold a black servant as an indefinite slave until 1670. In that year, the colonial assembly passed legislation permitting free whites, blacks, and Indians the right to own blacks as slaves. By 1699, the number of free blacks prompted fears of a "Negro insurrection." Virginia Colonial ordered the repatriation of freed blacks back to Africa. Many blacks sold themselves to white masters so they would not have to go to Africa. This was the first effort to gently repatriate free blacks back to Africa. The modern nations of Sierra Leone and Liberia both originated as colonies of repatriated former black slaves. However black slave owners continued to thrive in the United States. By 1830 there were 3,775 black families living in the South who owned black slaves. By 1860 there were about 3,000 slaves owned by black households in the city of New Orleans alone.[3]

African American historian John Hope Franklin writes:

The majority of Negro owners of slaves had some personal interest in their property. But, there were instances, however, in which free Negroes had a real economic interest in the institution of slavery and held slaves in order to improve their economic status. Without doubt, there were those who possessed slaves for the purpose of advancing their [own] well-being. . . . These Negro slaveholders were more interested in making their farms or carpenter-shops "pay" than they were in treating their slaves humanely. . . . There was some effort to conform to the pattern established by the dominant slaveholding group within the State in the effort to elevate themselves to a position of respect and privilege.[4]

Free black slave owners in New Orleans offered their services to the Confederacy and vowed to shed their blood in defense of their slave-owning ways. They even formed a black militia that numbered one thousand volunteers who fought for the Confederacy when the war broke out. This platoon would ultimately become the first Civil War unit to appoint black officers.

In 1830 around 321,000 individuals (14 percent) of the black population were free. These free blacks owned 13,000 slaves, which is almost nothing compared to the other 2 million slaves owned by white people. So who were some of the more prominent free black slave owners? John Carruthers Stanly had been born a slave in Craven County, North

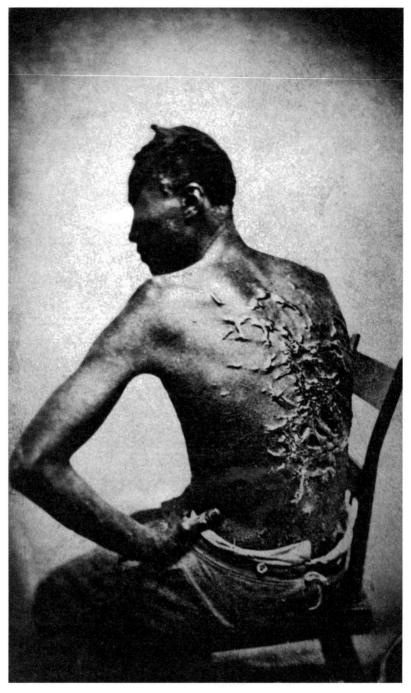

Fig. 7.1. A whipped Louisiana slave, 1863.
Baton Rouge, Louisiana, National Archives

Carolina, but graduated to become a freeman and one of America's first successful barbers. He parlayed his earnings into real estate, and by the early 1820s Stanly was the proud owner of three plantations and 163 slaves. He even hired white overseers to manage his properties!

William Ellison was the wealthiest black slave owner in South Carolina, a cotton gin maker and blacksmith who by the time of his death in 1860 owned one thousand acres of land and sixty-three slaves. From 1830 to 1865, Ellison and his sons were the only free blacks in Sumter County, South Carolina, to own slaves. During the Civil War they supported the Confederacy with substantial donations and aid. About 42 percent of free blacks owned slaves in Charleston, South Carolina, and surprisingly about 64 percent of these slaveholders were women.

By 1830, in Louisiana, several black people there owned a large number of slaves, including the following: In Pointe Coupee Parish alone, Sophie Delhonde owned 38 slaves; Lefroix Decuire owned 59 slaves; Antoine Decuire owned 70 slaves; Leandre Severin owned 60 slaves; and Victor Duperon owned 10. In St. John the Baptist Parish, Victoire Deslondes owned 52 slaves; in Plaquemine Brule, Martin Donatto owned 75 slaves; in Bayou Teche, Jean B. Muillion owned 52 slaves; Martin Lenormand in St. Martin Parish owned 44 slaves; Verret Polen in West Baton Rouge Parish owned 69 slaves; Francis Jerod in Washita Parish owned 33 slaves; and Cecee McCarty in the Upper Suburbs of New Orleans owned 32 slaves. Incredibly, the 13 members of the Metoyer family in Natchitoches Parish—including Nicolas Augustin Metoyer—collectively owned 215 slaves. Antoine Dubuclet and his wife Claire Pollard owned more than 70 slaves in Iberville Parish when they married. According to Thomas Clarkin, by 1864, in the midst of the Civil War, they owned 100 slaves, worth $94,700. During Reconstruction, he became the state's first black treasurer, serving between 1868 and 1878.

Andrew Durnford was a sugar planter and a physician who

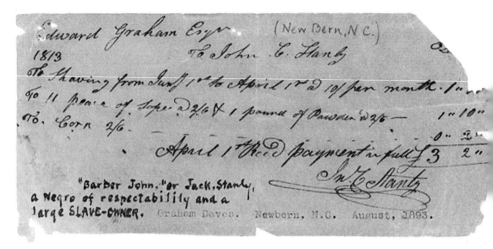

Fig. 7.2. A receipt for slaves belonging to John Carruthers Stanly, who had been born a slave but became a free black man who ironically decided to own slaves. He was, in fact, one of the largest slave owners in Craven County, North Carolina. Graham Daves Collection, North Carolina Archives

owned the St. Rosalie plantation, 33 miles south of New Orleans. In the late 1820s, David O. Whitten tells us, he paid $7,000 for seven male slaves, five females, and two children. He traveled all the way to Virginia in the 1830s and purchased 24 more. Eventually, he would own 77 slaves. When a fellow Creole slave owner liberated 85 of his slaves and shipped them off to Liberia, Durnford commented that he couldn't do that, because "self-interest is too strongly rooted in the bosom of all that breathes the American atmosphere."[5]

By the eve of the Civil War the phenomenon of free blacks owning slaves had almost disappeared except in the lower South and places such as Louisiana. The practice of slavery is one of the world's oldest vices, sometimes even a color-blind affair. Owning another person, black or white, male or female, is an evil business. Using the immoral practice of slavery as the main rallying cry for war, the Rothschild bankers were once again on the invisible front lines prepping for battle. In 1854 they had been instrumental in financing a key Southern Masonic outfit known as the Knights of the Golden Circle (KGC), which was

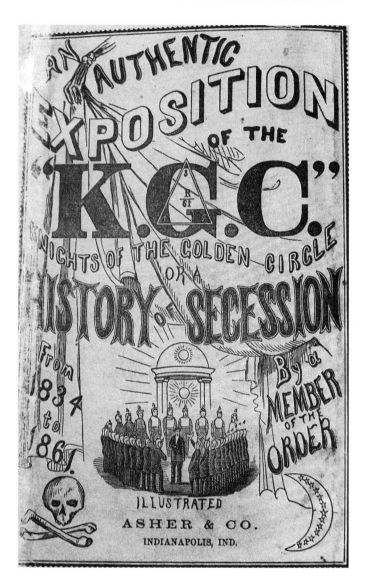

Fig. 7.3. Knights of the Golden Circle pamphlet (1861)

formed to ignite racial and political tensions associated with the issue of slavery. Prominent members of this secret society included Lincoln assassin John Wilkes Booth, Confederate president Jefferson Davis, and the Confederate secretary of war, Judah P. Benjamin. After their defeat in the Civil War, Benjamin and cronies escaped with as much gold from the Confederacy's Treasury as they could, packed it on a boat, and shipped it back to England to the Rothschilds. The rest of the gold, more than two million dollars' worth, was divided up, stashed away, and over time essentially lost to the history books.

The Rothschilds controlled England via Lionel Rothschild while his brother James controlled the finances of France, making the Rothschilds once again masters of the chessboard playing both sides. Their concerns regarding America were openly written about in the Rothschild-owned *Times of London*.

> If that mischievous financial policy, which had its origin in the North American Republic [i.e., honest constitutionally authorized no-debt money], should become indurated down to a fixture, then that government will furnish its own money without cost. It will pay off its debts and be without a debt [to the international bankers]. It will become prosperous beyond precedent in the history of the civilized governments of the world. The brains and wealth of all countries will go to North America. That government must be destroyed or it will destroy every monarchy on the globe.[6]

The Rothschilds and their agents conspired with local politicians, bankers, and those in power to work against the best interests of America. Their carefully spun propaganda and shady behind-the-scenes meddling advanced into open rebellion and secession as, on December 29, 1860, South Carolina became the first Southern state to break free of the Union. Within weeks six more states had joined the fray, likewise pulling away from the Union to form the Confederate States of America and naming Jefferson Davis as their president. These Confederate plotters began raiding army surpluses and seizing forts, weapons, coined currency, and many other valuable properties belonging to the Union. President Buchanan's cabinet wasn't very loyal to the Union either and was close to bankrupting the nation, while ignoring the secession and blatant Confederate naval attacks on Union batteries in South Carolina.

Shortly thereafter Abraham Lincoln became president and was

inaugurated on March 4, 1861. Buchanan left a burning fire of hell for Lincoln to step into as the fifty-one-year-old mound-and-giant enthusiast took office a mere month before the start of the Civil War. When in office Lincoln immediately ordered a blockade of European supplies to Southern ports, a move that inadvertently kicked off the war as the Confederates took the bold step of sacking Fort Sumter on April 12, 1861.

The war was on, and the Rothschilds were licking their lips. By Thanksgiving large numbers of British, French, and Spanish troops started amassing in Mexico while resources and aid to the Confederacy began pouring in from Europe. If the Rothschilds' motivation for starting the Civil War was to kill a good chunk of Americans and then take back the U.S. banking system, they were off to a good start.

They had managed to get control of most of the banks in New York. This was thanks to their agent August Belmont, who had decades' worth of banking experience behind him as well as deep Rothschild connections, formed by working for both the Frankfurt and Naples branches of their empire. Belmont's wife was the niece of John Slidell, a partner with Judah P. Benjamin in a law firm in New Orleans. Slidell was also a commissary sent to France to purchase supplies and ammunition for the Confederacy. Another branch of the Rothschild tree—the Lehman family—got their start by smuggling arms to the South and cotton to the North. The Rothschilds desired to produce chaotic conditions in America in the hopes of breaking up the fragile country. A united debt-free America was too powerful for them to contend with, but a splintered nation lunging at each other's throats was a recipe made in heaven. Their old trick of supporting both sides at once increased their chances for victory.

In New York, August Belmont shared valuable information with influential financiers in England and France while fellow agent Salomon James Rothschild helped finance the Confederate army. Salomon was a well-traveled playboy banker who had enjoyed extensive tours of philandering through America, Canada, and Cuba and was an eyewitness

Fig. 7.4. Bombardment of Fort Sumter (1861) by Currier & Ives

Fig. 7.5. Paris estate of Salomon Rothschild by Sigoise

to the events leading up to the Civil War. Salomon was a representative of the world's most prominent banking family and traveled with an entourage that mingled solely with high society.

Salomon was also a pornography addict as noted by prominent New York lawyer and diarist George Templeton Strong, who met Salomon at a "carriage parade" party in Central Park and then again at the New York Club before Salomon was indefinitely banned from the vaunted establishment for lewd behavior. Strong wrote, "The Baron, though illustrious and a millionaire, was immoderately given to lewd talk and nude photographs."[7] Salomon later married one of his cousins, keeping the money in the family bloodline, a practice typical of the elites. However, he didn't live long enough to enjoy it, because he died unexpectedly two years later in Paris at the young age of twenty-nine. The famous French writers the Goncourt brothers wrote, "Cabarrus, the Rothschild's doctor, told Saint-Victor that the young Rothschild who died the other day really died of the excitement of gambling on the stock exchange."[8] This was a fitting end to the life of a Rothschild. Salomon's views, concerns, and opinions on the Civil War, as revealed in the following letter, are fascinating. Especially interesting is the section about using his family influence in support of the Confederacy.

New Orleans, April 28, '61

I am writing you a separate letter on politics, which is even more confused here than in Europe, but I cannot recommend to you strongly enough to use every influence of our family and our friends to have the Republic of the Southern Confederacy recognized as soon as possible. You will tell me that my ideas have changed, but when you read my other letter, you will tell me I am right, for in this way bloodshed and an immense destruction of property would be stopped. I have been in New Orleans for a month now, and I had expected to spend only a few days here. But the political events, which followed one another with such rapidity, were of such a throbbing interest to me that I thought it was my duty to prolong my stay and to make a thoroughgoing study of this very difficult and delicate matter. Having stayed in the North and in the South, having heard all possible discussions in favor of and against each side, I had the leisure to form a completely independent opinion of my own. I am going to try to transmit it to you, though it is difficult to do so in writing. Therefore, I should start a little farther back.

You know that the former United States was made up of two great parties, the Democrats and the Republicans. These two parties were subdivided into groups, few in numbers, but extremely violent. The abolitionists were the ultra-Republicans; the "fire-eaters" or secessionists, the ultra-Democrats. Fanaticism and extreme factions always carry things their way, and as I gave you a presentiment a long time ago, abolition on the one side and secession on the other won over the moderate neutrals, in spite of themselves. The point of departure, then, as you know, was the question of slavery. Naturally, since this institution is the source of the wealth of the South, it was defended to the utmost by those who derived profit from it. Two reasons impelled the inhabitants of the North to seek the destruction of slavery by all possible means.

The first, which was given by those who wanted to deceive, to win over, chivalrous hearts and to lure European sympathies, was a simple reason, that of humanity. In a free country like America, there shouldn't be any slaves, and complete equality should prevail among all classes. The proof that this reason was not sincere is that the abolitionists spent millions in order to incite insurrections among the slaves, or to induce them to flee from their masters, but let them die of hunger because they were free, and gave them no opportunity for moral advancement. However, the real sentiment, which guided them and which they did not dare admit in that moment, was that feeling of leveling whereby everybody would have to be nominally equal. They couldn't bear to see the inhabitants of the South with two hundred hands at their service, when they each had only two hands themselves. This feeling was the first germ of the social revolution, which is now swiftly following the political revolution.

You will recall that I have been talking to you about this for a long time. The South had numerous sympathizers in the North, but these sympathizers were more interested than it was believed; they knew that with the help of the southern states they could keep power. This state of affairs could have continued for many years if the two divisions, South and North, of the Democratic Party had not split at the last electoral convention. Since each of them carried a different candidate, they surrendered power to a third thief, Lincoln, the Republican choice. The cotton states understood that there was no longer any security for them in a union in which the chief of state and all his ministers were their most implacable enemies. They seceded. Unfortunately for them, the secession was carried out, as everything is done on this continent, illegally and boastfully; and their bravado alienated many moderate men from them and prevented the central slave states from joining them right away. The Republican administration, thinking that it was dealing with just a small number of states without a large population, and supposing that within these very states the Unionist feeling was still very much alive and was silent only because of the violence and coercion of some demagogic ringleaders, resorted to repressive measures, for which the Constitution of the United States gave no authorization at all.

The first effect of these measures was to make the sentiment for secession unanimous in the gulf states and strongly to estrange the central states. The latter made a last effort to bring the two factions together, but failed on both sides. After having promised the evacuation of Fort Sumter, the administration tried to resupply it. Several warships appeared in the roadstead; the population of Charlestown was aroused and, perhaps in too much haste, bombarded the fort and captured it. This first cannon shot decided the question. Lincoln issued a proclamation ordering the *rebels* to disband within twenty days and to raise the flag of the United States again under penalty of being punished and coerced by force of arms. The situation was becoming clear. The entire Deep South was united; the North was beginning to be, but it still had within its ranks many persons who favored southern rights. Pecuniary interests did the rest.

The great question over which the representatives of the South and those of the North had been locked in bitter combat for thirty years was the question of tariffs. The South was a producer of raw materials and a consumer; the North was a manufacturer. Free trade, or at least very moderate custom duties, was the desire of the inhabitants of the South. The North was contending in favor of protection, often even of the prohibition [of imports]. By the old tariff law, the eastern states and New England furnished the other states merchandise, which these latter could procure in Europe, at reductions of twenty-five and thirty percent. As soon as the Republican administration (the protector of tariffs) came to power, Congress passed the Morrill Tariff, which raised duties to an unprecedented rate. The states that had seceded responded with a very great decrease in these same tariffs, intimating their eventual, complete abolition when the peaceful state of the country should allow them freedom from recourse to extraordinary measures. The North understood that it was lost if secession continued and made progress. Who would then come to buy the iron products of Pennsylvania and the manufactured goods of New England? It would no longer be the South, for the South would get its supplies in the European markets and would find a way to pass its purchases into the western states.

From that moment on, the South no longer had a supporter in the North; Republicans and Democrats crowded around the flag of the Union. Patriotism and the old memories played some part in this; but believe me, the principal motive was the pocket. It was therefore necessary to get rid, at all cost, of this spirit of revolt, which was making daily progress and bringing the North closer to its ruin. The western and eastern states offered their troops and their treasuries to the government, and were willing to go to any extreme of sacrifice, but this appeal reverberated in a different way in the states that had as yet not decided. Virginia seceded immediately and, bringing to the Southern Confederacy the help of her numerous population and of her inexhaustible storehouses, sought to make up for lost time by seizing the federal arsenals. Tennessee and Kentucky answered that they didn't have a single man to aid the administration to coerce the states of the South, but that they would find a hundred thousand men to defend them. Governor [C. F.] Jackson of Missouri, who was not counted on at all, for that state is surrounded by abolitionist populations and is only half slave, answered Lincoln "that his request was illegal, unconstitutional, . . . and diabolical." Maryland also revolted, and the federal troops had to make their way through Baltimore amidst a rain of paving stones, which killed some of them and wounded many more.[9]

Although stressing the importance of backing the South, the Rothschilds also backed the North and hoped for a long war and an eventual stalemate. They fanned the sparks of war knowing that they would reap a golden harvest once they divided the country in half. They foresaw no other conclusion than the American government begging them for financial help, which in turn the only solution they'd offer would be another rechartering of a Rothschild-owned central bank. At that time foreign financiers like the Rothschilds still owned the majority of state banks that had popped up after Biddle's Second Bank collapse. By loaning money to these state banks at high interest rates the Rothschilds were able to control almost all of the loan decisions that were being made; these loans were typically backed by state bonds.

The state of Mississippi, for example, sold $5 million in bonds with which to subscribe a third of the $15 million capital of the Union Bank. The promoters of the Union Bank made ill-advised loans and within a short time the bank failed. The state officials in Mississippi realized that the foreign financiers had hoped to reap windfall profits and had been largely responsible for the failure of the Union Bank, so these officials refused to repay the money owed the foreign vultures. The European financiers bought up "repudiated" southern state bonds and then began to use their financial power to have the United States federal government compel the southern states to pay off the disputed claims. The Rothschilds and the other foreign financier groups also thought they might be able to use their money power to force the U.S. federal government to assume the debts of the southern state banks as federal obligations. At its inception, the newly formed United States had assumed the debts of the colonies; so the foreign vultures thought they might be able to force the federal government to pay off the southern states' debts. The issue of "states' rights" versus a "strong central authority" became a national crisis point and the American Civil War was the result. War is a very profitable stratagem for rulers. The Rothschilds and other European financiers exacerbated the discord and hostility between the North and the South. Knowing full well that war was their best means of reaping huge profits, these vultures did everything in their power to instigate an American Civil War.[10]

By 1861, America was $100 million in debt, and its new president, Abraham Lincoln, had no choice but to seek financial help from the Rothschilds. With their plan working to perfection, they welcomed him with huge smiles and open arms.

8
Abraham Lincoln Discovers the Truth

1862–1865

Daughter of Isis

I do not forget
I too will comply
As will the universe
With the coming reply
First row deceivers
Slave class pretenders
Priestesses
Cathars, Goths and Jesuits
Surrender
Here is the thrill
Of all that is real
Knowing the deal
Is a flame at the heel
That we're all facing together
This wild new unknown
I am the daughter of Isis
My time has come
For in the hour of crisis
You wanted me home

ESTRELLA EGUINO

139

*Get your facts first, and then you can distort them as much
as you please.*

MARK TWAIN

The war years of 1862 and 1863 were tough on the president given that
the cost of keeping his war going was sinking the nation into bank-
ruptcy. With no alternative in sight, he was forced to seek financial aid
from the Rothschilds. Lincoln's giant stature and immediate charisma
was duly noted by the bankers as they dined on beef stroganoff and
popcorn balls. Lincoln had recently made Thanksgiving a national holi-
day, and they toasted to their forefathers and the end of the war. But
the Rothschilds weren't interested in ending the war—at least not until
their central bank had been rechartered. This was a topic they discussed
with passion as they laid out the terms of their deal to a heavyhearted
Lincoln.

The deal wasn't a sweet one. The Rothschilds agreed to provide
Lincoln the currency he needed at 35 percent interest on all monies
loaned as long as they were allowed a new charter for another United
States central bank. Lincoln held a poker face during the meeting and
once it ended told them that he would be in touch. What Lincoln
did next made the Rothschilds angrier than Jackson had made them.
Recognizing the Rothschild hijacking for what it was, and furious about
the high level of interest they attempted to gain from him, Lincoln
made his boldest presidential move yet—he printed his own debt-free
money. Called "the greenback," these bills were essentially the proto-
type for what modern American currency became: smallish green bills
that were easy to carry.

During a meeting in Chicago, Lincoln's friend Colonel Edmund
Dick Taylor had mentioned the idea of creating a new currency to pay
for the war. Taylor was a friend of Andrew Jackson's and was well versed
in Rothschild economics. He was also a Northern slave owner from
Illinois who had made a fortune in the coal-mining business. He, like a

Fig. 8.1. Abraham Lincoln poses in photographer Alexander Gardner's new studio gallery in Washington, D.C., on November 8, 1863. This image was sold at auction by Sotheby's for $98,500 in 2011. PH Filing Series Photograph Collection, Library of Congress

lot of Northerners in 1863, was worried that the South might actually win the war.

Based on Taylor's suggestions Lincoln intentionally ignored the Rothschilds by authorizing Congress to print the greenbacks as full legal Treasury tender. Lincoln flooded the economy with $450 million of the new currency, which was distinguished from all other currencies by the green ink on the back of the bills. The money was a godsend. Soldiers got paid, and the economy boomed, though Lincoln was greatly concerned at having to issue fiat-based currency backed by nothing. He declared, "We gave the people of this republic the greatest blessing they ever had, their own paper money to pay their own debts."[1] Lincoln did this despite knowing the gargantuan risks involved.

As the Rothschilds fumed over being betrayed and decided what actions to take, Lincoln introduced state loans that the nefarious bankers couldn't touch, thus financing the Civil War on state-issued credit. Fearing a wicked response, Lincoln slept with one eye open as he fought the bankers over the greenbacks and a proposed American national banking system. He also freed the slaves with his Emancipation Proclamation—a move that infuriated the Rothschilds even more and crippled the South's economic future.

But Lincoln couldn't truly escape the Rothschilds, at least not when it came to money. His personal banker, Jay Cooke, was hired to sell small government bonds to the average citizen, but instead he sold them in London and hired more than twenty-five hundred subagents who hawked over a billion dollars' worth of bonds in three years. Cooke was

Fig. 8.2. Lincoln's greenback. National Numismatic Collection, National Museum of American History

Fig. 8.3. *First Reading of the Emancipation Proclamation of President Lincoln* by Francis Bicknell Carpenter (1864), on display at the United States Capitol

later forced to pay the Treasury back after getting caught backroom dealing with the Rothschilds and J. P. Morgan.

But as reelection neared, Lincoln had control over both Congress and America's banking system, and he enacted measures to keep the Rothschilds in check. These took the form of the National Banking Acts of 1863 and 1864. Lincoln's measures included a nationally regulated private banking system intent on issuing cheap credit to build industries that were not reliant on the Southern plantation system.

The office of Comptroller of the Currency was established. No National Banking Association could start business without his certificate of authorization. He could at any time appoint investigators to look into the affairs of any national bank. Regulations covered minimum capitalization, reserve requirements, the definition of bad debts, reporting on financial condition and identity of ownership, and other elements of safety to depositors. Every bank director had to be an American citizen, and three-quarters of a bank's directors had to be residents of the state in which the bank did business. Each bank was limited in the interest rate it could charge by the strictures of its state's usury laws; or if none were in effect, then to 7 percent. If it were caught exceeding this limitation, it would forfeit the loan in question and would have to refund to the victimized borrower twice what he had paid in interest. Banks could not hold real estate for more than five years, aside from bank buildings. A national bank had to deposit with the Treasury, U.S. bonds amounting to at least one third of its capital. It would receive in return government-printed notes, which it could circulate as money. Thus the banks would have to lend the government substantial sums for the war effort to qualify for federal charters, and a sound currency would be circulated to the public for an expanding economy.

Meanwhile, national banks could not circulate notes printed by themselves. In order to eliminate all competition with the new national currency, the notes of state-chartered banks were hit with a massive tax in the following year. Most large commercial banks organized themselves according to the new system, and many new large banks were formed, as national banks. Despite historically unprecedented financing needs, the government raised and printed the cash to fight and win the Civil War. With the combination of banking, tariff, educational, and agricultural measures enacted under Abraham Lincoln, the United States began the greatest period of industrial development ever seen.[2]

Lincoln's financial reform plans were working, and he proposed that they become permanent policy. The money changers in London were furious at this. Furthermore, their war efforts on behalf of their Southern investments weren't panning out either as new industrial inventions like machine guns began to obliterate the South's chances of winning the contest. To combat Lincoln's paper money experiment and the impending end of the Civil War, the Rothschilds surrounded

Fig. 8.4. Caricature of Lincoln and Russian tsar Alexander II standing as friends by Rufus Rockwell Wilson (1863)

America's borders with foreign troops waiting to swoop in and prolong the conflict with a planned military invasion.

The British were situated up north in Canada with more than eleven thousand troops waiting to invade New York, while both France and Spain had united in Mexico with another thirty thousand soldiers willing to carve up America on the Rothschilds' bidding. Jefferson Davis even offered Louisiana and Texas to France in exchange for their military support against the North. But the money masters' intricately planned two-sided attack was thwarted by Tsar Alexander II of Russia, the only European monarch not indebted to the Rothschilds' banking empire.

Russia shared a good economic relationship with America, which had inspired them to end serfdom and emulate the American practice of private farming. Russia even copied the modern construction methods of the U.S. Navy and by 1864 had built the third largest fleet of ships

Fig. 8.5. Russian tsar Alexander II sends the Russian fleet to New York Harbor and to San Pablo Bay, California (shown here), in 1863, to defend Lincoln's Union from the pro-Confederacy British and French imperial powers. *Harper's Weekly* (1864); the Schiller Institute

Fig. 8.6. The Russian squadron in the harbor of New York, October 1863, on a supposed secret mission by special arrangement with the federal government, from Frank Leslie's *The Soldier in Our Civil War* (1893). Russiannobility.org

in the world, trailing only behind Britain and France. When Lincoln learned that Alexander II had also rejected the Rothschilds' continual attempts to set up a central bank in Russia he saw that the two leaders were in the same boat, and so he asked for the tsar's help during the Civil War. The tsar obliged and sent his fleet across the Atlantic with a specific warning to the Rothschilds that an attack on America would be considered an attack on Russia as well.

Now at Lincoln's disposal, the tsar's Russian fleet steamed in to New York Harbor on September 24, 1863; his Pacific fleet anchored in San Francisco a few weeks later. Lincoln's secretary of the navy, Gideon Wells, wrote in his diary, "They arrived at the high tide of the Confederacy and the low tide of the North, causing England and France to hesitate long enough to turn the tide for the North."[3] This deliberate naval move by the tsar and his Russian fleet prevented France and Britain from carrying out their invasion plans given that the Rothschilds weren't ready to risk war with Russia. The British and French troops that had amassed on America's borders waited in vain to repossess the wealth of the colonies, but while they waited their moment slipped away as the war ended and Lincoln was declared the victor.

In 1864, now considered a public hero, Lincoln was easily reelected president as he vowed to further strengthen the economy without the aid of foreign banks. Under those circumstances the Rothschilds ditched their plans to destroy America and once again sailed home with their tails between their legs. Thanks to Lincoln's greenbacks and Tsar Alexander II's fleet, America had defeated them for the third time. But Lincoln wouldn't be around long enough to enjoy his victory as the reaper marched toward him a spooky seven days after the Civil War ended on May 9, 1865.

On April 11, 1865, a cool Tuesday evening, the radiantly illuminated White House was host to a vast crowd of people assembled to hear Lincoln speak. Throughout the city bonfires blazed, parades rolled by, and rockets whistled through the air, welcoming the celebratory news of Robert E. Lee's surrender to Ulysses S. Grant at Appomattox two days earlier. The people were anxious to hear the great emancipator's speech. Lincoln was a famous orator, thanks to his iconic Gettysburg Address.

As darkness fell, lights illuminated the city. At the War Department every window was glowing with light and the building decorated with large flags. The north portico of the White House was also brightly lit. Men and women gathered and stood in ankle-deep mud from the April rains. They not only filled the grounds in front of the White House but spilled over onto the sidewalks from Fifteenth to Seventeenth Streets. Banners streamed and bands played.

At last Lincoln appeared and was greeted with "tremendous and continued applause." Mrs. Lincoln and some friends could be seen in an adjoining window. Noah Brooks, the Washington correspondent for the *Sacramento Daily Union,* observed later that "there was something terrible about the enthusiasm with which the beloved Chief Magistrate was received—cheers upon cheers, wave after wave of applause rolled up, the President modestly standing quiet until it was over."

Writing several years afterward, Mary Todd Lincoln's black seamstress Elizabeth Keckley recalled a vast mass of heads like "a black, gently swelling sea. . . . Close to the White House the faces were plainly discernible, but they faded into mere ghostly outlines on the outskirts of the assembly; and what added to the weird, spectral beauty of the scene, was the confused hum of voices that rose above the sea of forms"*
Lincoln began his speech without knowing it would be his last. "We meet this evening, not in sorrow, but in gladness of heart,"[4] Petersburg and Richmond had been evacuated. Only a week earlier the president had walked through the streets of Richmond and had sat in Jefferson Davis's chair at the Confederate White House. Lee's army had surrendered. On March 4, the war still was not over; on April 11, it essentially was. Lincoln not only sought justice, he also desired mercy.

Mercy wouldn't be in the cards for Lincoln, though, and his final

---

*http://etc.usf.edu/lit2go/87/behind-the-scenes/1468/chapter-11-the-assassination-of
-president-lincoln

Fig. 8.7. John Wilkes Booth in Masonic pose

speech became a dud to the press who were disappointed about his war-time reconstruction views and his willingness to forgive the South with immediate reentry back into the Union. As Lincoln spoke two members of the Southern Masonic crew Knights of the Golden Circle—John Wilkes Booth and Lewis Powell—dillydallied near the front of the White House grounds, sickened by what they'd heard and itching to put an end to the tall man's reign. Booth tried to convince Powell to shoot Lincoln during the speech, but Powell smartly refused. As the speech ended and everyone went home, Booth promised, "That is the last speech he will ever make," a threat he made good three days later.

But this Booth was neither a Southerner nor a slave owner. He was, in fact, the greatest and most respected actor of his day. And in the

Fig. 8.8. John Wilkes Booth the actor/assassin. Biography.com

era before selfies, Twitter, and instant narcissistic satisfaction he sought to be a hero, immortal—not a madman, but a conqueror of moral justice for the people. Intent on restoring glory to the South and forever etching his name in the history books, Booth viewed his final act as the nation's saving grace. His name would, of course, be permanently embedded in the annals of American history, although not in the manner in which he had hoped.

As Booth the assassin entered Ford's Theatre on April 15, 1865, he found no secret service to greet him. Nor was Lincoln's private security guard there either; he was too busy getting hammered at the pub across the street to be worried about some rich actor. But Booth was more than an actor, he was a cultured, well-traveled intellect; a Master Mason; and friend of the Rothschilds. In fact, they couldn't have hired a better assassin.

As Booth peeked in the tiny peephole that separated him from Lincoln's private presidential balcony box seats he realized there was nothing and no one to prevent him from entering. And so he entered quietly, timing his attack to coincide with a scene from the play that was guaranteed to elicit a loud ripple of laughter from the audience.

Booth had studied the play and knew exactly when the noise of the

THE ASSASSINATION OF PRESIDENT LINCOLN,
AT FORD'S THEATRE WASHINGTON,D.C.APRIL 14TH 1865.

Fig. 8.9. Depiction of Lincoln's assassination by Currier & Ives

audience was expected to be at its highest, thereby providing the perfect silencer as he pulled out his six-inch, .44-caliber derringer and aimed it at the back of Lincoln's head. Lincoln had seen Booth perform as the villain of the French play *The Marble Heart* in 1863, a play in which Booth had directed all of his anger and fierce lines right at Lincoln sitting in his presidential box seats.

Lincoln had also almost met the wrath of Booth a mere six weeks earlier when, on the day of Lincoln's second inauguration, March 5, 1865, Booth had positioned himself behind the scaffolds that had been set up in the Capitol Rotunda. Waiting for Lincoln to emerge from the Senate chamber to deliver his second inaugural address, Booth was stopped by a concerned citizen who noticed a crazed look in his eye. Booth backed off from shooting Lincoln on that day but still decided to hang around long enough to photobomb the president in the only known photograph of the event.

It seems that murder had been on Booth's mind for quite a few

Fig. 8.10. Booth (upper circled image) at Lincoln's second inaugural address. Civilwartalk.com

weeks, and now, with his derringer aimed at Lincoln at point-blank range, the moment of reckoning was at hand. As the audience laughed on cue, Booth fired a single shot to the back of Lincoln's head.

The bullet entered near the president's left ear and lodged behind his eyeball, instantly paralyzing him. In less than twenty-four hours Lincoln would become the first American president to have been assassinated, and John Wilkes Booth would be the subject of the greatest manhunt in history. But Booth's legendary tale was only just beginning, and the greatest actor of his time was setting the stage for a mysterious final disappearing act. Booth's life, both before and after the Lincoln murder, was a "play" of epic proportions, consisting of conspiracy theories too wild to be true and a family history with links to—you guessed it—the Rothschilds.

9
Assassin's Creed: John Wilkes Booth

1865–?

The Hero and the Madman

*Are you the one
That I think you are?
If I recall you're the actor
Who took to the stage
Set the world ablaze
With your anger and your rage
With every new leaf
You turned and wrote a new page
Cleverly concealing
Your real age
Those that knew you
Were always quite amazed
Are you the one
Who can take this praise?
Are you the hero or are you the madman?*

PHILIP LYNOTT

When the power of love overcomes the love of power the world will know peace.

JIMI HENDRIX

April of 1865 was a wild month in America. Blacks were free, the Civil War was over, and the president was dead. The nation was in shock, much like they would be nearly a hundred years later when John F. Kennedy met the same fate, although the latter president's death was much more spectacular because it was broadcast on national television. Lincoln shared some striking similarities with JFK. They were both elected to Congress and became president exactly one hundred years apart from each other. Below is a partial list of strange similarities and other oddities concerning the two presidential greats.

- Lincoln was elected to Congress in 1846; John F. Kennedy was elected to Congress in 1946.
- Lincoln was elected president in 1860; John F. Kennedy was elected president in 1960.
- Both were champions of civil rights.
- Both had a child die while they were living in the White House.
- Both presidents were shot in the back of the head on a Friday.
- Both of their successors were named Johnson.
- Andrew Johnson, who succeeded Lincoln, was born in 1808; Lyndon B. Johnson, who succeeded Kennedy, was born in 1908.
- An assassination plot against Lincoln was uncovered by a New York police chief named John Kennedy.
- Lincoln was shot at Ford's Theatre; Kennedy was shot in a Lincoln limousine, a product of Ford.
- Lincoln's presidential seats were in box 7 of Ford's Theatre; Kennedy rode in Ford car number 7 of the Dallas motorcade.
- Both autopsies were performed by military personnel.
- Mrs. Kennedy (Jackie Onassis) insisted that JFK's funeral mirror Lincoln's.
- Both assassins were murdered before they could tell their version of the story to the public.
- Both assassins were also detained by a man named Baker, and

both were eventually killed by a single shot from a Colt revolver.

- Both assassins were killed by other assassins who had both changed their names. The soldier Boston Corbett (Thomas Corbett) shot Booth in a glowing burning barn; Jack Ruby (Jacob Rubenstein) killed Oswald in front of the glowing lights of the press.

- Booth ran from a theater only to be caught in a warehouse.

- Oswald ran from a warehouse and was caught in a theater.

When JFK was murdered on national television there were only three channels to cover the story; a hundred years prior television didn't exist and the Internet was still a prophetic fantasy floating around in Nikola Tesla's head. It's safe to say that news traveled pretty slowly in 1865. So despite having just murdered the president, Booth had plenty of time in which to make his escape. It was a hampered one, being that he broke his leg jumping from the theater balcony after shooting Lincoln. He also had a pretty wicked knife tussle with Major Henry Rathbone, who, with his stepsister/girlfriend Clara Harris, was accompanying the president to the play.

After the assassination these two eyewitnesses to Lincoln's killing were sent to the mental ward for a significant amount of time. They would be released after a few months, and they eventually married; however, their sanity disappeared when Rathbone ended up shooting his wife in the face a few years later.

Lincoln's wife, Mary, was also present at her husband's assassination as Kennedy's wife had been when JFK was killed. Mary allegedly held her husband's head in agony and disbelief after Booth had shot him. Lincoln probably wasn't that surprised, however, as it's widely believed he anticipated his assassination. He even spoke about the reoccurring violent dreams he had been having, telling his friend and Lincoln biographer Ward Hill Lamon about one of them three days before his assassination.

About ten days ago, I retired very late. I had been up waiting for important dispatches from the front. I could not have been long in bed when I fell into a slumber, for I was weary. I soon began to dream. There seemed to be a deathlike stillness about me. Then I heard subdued sobs, as if a number of people were weeping. I thought I left my bed and wandered downstairs. There the silence was broken by the same pitiful sobbing, but the mourners were invisible. I went from room to room; no living person was in sight, but the same mournful sounds of distress met me as I passed along. I saw light in all the rooms; every object was familiar to me; but where were all the people who were grieving as if their hearts would break?

I was puzzled and alarmed. What could be the meaning of all this? Determined to find the cause of a state of things so mysterious and so shocking, I kept on until I arrived at the East Room, which I entered. There I met with a sickening surprise. Before me was a catafalque on which rested a corpse wrapped in funeral vestments. Around it were stationed soldiers who were acting as guards; and there was a throng of people, gazing mournfully upon the corpse, whose face was covered, others weeping pitifully. "Who is dead in the White House?" I demanded of one of the soldiers, "The President," was his answer; "he was killed by an assassin." Then came a loud burst of grief from the crowd, which woke me from my dream. I slept no more that night; and although it was only a dream, I have been strangely annoyed by it ever since.[1]

On the day of his assassination Lincoln told his bodyguard that for three straight nights he had dreamed of being assassinated! Yet he dismissed his bodyguard and all other security agents on that fateful night of April 15. On this night he was shot in in the back of his head near the left side of his ear, while Major Rathbone, the old war hero, jumped into immediate action, attempting to thwart Booth after the shooting. But Booth pulled his bowie knife and slashed Rathbone across the arm before jumping off the balcony while screaming a Latin war cry. When

Booth landed, he felt his leg crunch upon impact. He hobbled out of the theater in search of his horse after running past throngs of shocked playgoers in the audience. Booth even attempted to stab the orchestral leader, who had foolishly reached out to subdue him.

I've always wondered why Booth would choose to use a tiny, one-shot derringer pistol for the deed. After all, six-shot revolvers were plentiful; one could buy one at any gun shop in the city.

The derringer was considered a girl's gun.

Curiously enough, Lincoln's wife, Mary, also carried a derringer; hers was a fancy, white-handled one that she loved to show off by waving it around town. She was also left-handed, and Lincoln was shot on the left side of his head, which would have been a trickier shot considering that she was sitting on his right side.

Fig. 9.1. John Wilkes Booth

Fig. 9.2. Broadside advertising reward for capture of Lincoln assassination conspirators. Illustrated with photographic prints of John H. Surratt, John Wilkes Booth, and David E. Herold

Fig. 9.3. The Philadelphia Deringer pistol Booth used to murder Lincoln, on display at the museum in Ford's Theatre

Fig. 9.4. Mary Lincoln in 1861. Photo by Matthew Brady

Did Mary have a hand in killing Abraham Lincoln? She was discouraged from attending her husband's funeral or other postmortem services and eventually was denied her customary widow's pension despite repeated appeals. According to *The Addiction of Mary Todd Lincoln,* Mary had a dependence on opium and relied heavily on the drug, which was being supplied to the artists at Ford's Theatre by a drug-dealing, part-time actor. This unknown actor apparently looked like Booth—so much so that he would often double for him when Booth had multiple acting commitments in different cities.

The Rothschilds were still licking their wounds and had been desperate to remove the newly reelected Lincoln from office as quickly as possible. According to the *Bloodlines of the Illuminati* there's even a slight possibility that Lincoln was one of their own, sired illegitimately when Lincoln's mother worked as a maid for Rothschild kin. Events that transpired during Lincoln's early years are hard to verify one way or the other, but according to another story of the day Lincoln had sired a secret family, one with royal bloodlines. Accordingly, when he was a thirty-year-old lawyer who rode by horseback on the cold Illinois trails he met and had an affair with the illegitimate daughter of King Leopold of Hapsburg. He fathered two girls with her and had managed to keep this a secret his entire life. The Rothschilds hoped this information, when made public, would ruin the president. Thus they devised a plot to kidnap him to help set it in motion. They would kidnap him and then release him together with the information about his illegitimate family, hoping this would create a scandal and bring about his downfall.

If Mary suspected something about Abe's secret family, perhaps it was a motivating factor for her participation in his assassination. Remember, she was an opium addict. On the night of the assassination an empty carriage was seen at the back of Ford's Theatre. Was it intended to spirit away the kidnap victim? That would have made sense. But what was the plan? Was look-a-like Booth supposed to barge in and knock the president unconscious and then whisk away the body to be dumped into the empty carriage behind the theater and then taken to parts unknown? And let's assume for argument's sake that Mary Lincoln had signed off on this plan and was to be a willing accomplice of it, but what about Officer Rathbone, who had accompanied them to the play. What was look-a-like Booth supposed to do about him? Imagine the shock of Booth's look-alike when he entered the box to find Mary Lincoln skipping the kidnapping plot altogether and going straight into assassination mode. She pulled the trigger and slyly killed her husband while Booth's look-alike panicked, knowing his cronies were downstairs, waiting to spirit the president away. Booth's look-alike might then have realized that perhaps Mary had intended to kill her husband all along and that he (the look-alike) was the fall guy. With little time to think the assassin, with a quick knife slash, deflected Rathbone's attempt to grab him and boldly jumped off the balcony to the hard wooden floors ten feet below, breaking his leg in the process.

But according to eyewitness accounts the man fleeing across the stage didn't have a broken leg and held his bloody bowie knife in his right hand, seeming to indicate that he was right-handed. However, the bullet that killed Lincoln was definitely fired by a left-handed assailant as its trajectory entered diagonally through Lincoln's left ear, smashed through brain tissue, and ended up lodged behind his right eye.

According to all the early witness accounts, events played out very quickly, and the suspect was across the stage and out of the building before anyone realized what had happened. It was only then, when it was too late to apprehend the suspect, that Mary Lincoln's anguished cries from the box could be heard, along with Rathbone's futile exhortations to stop the fleeing suspect. But why did it take so long for Mary Todd and the others to cry out? Mary Lincoln had had her husband gunned down as he sat right beside her, hand in hand. She had then witnessed a violent struggle between her husband's killer and Major Rathbone, during which Rathbone was grievously wounded, slashed from shoulder to elbow bathing the box in blood.

Had Rathbone succumbed to his alleged wound, Mary and Clara would have been left alone in that box with a knife-wielding madman. You would think then that they would have been screaming bloody murder throughout the ordeal, and quite likely trying to exit that box. Help, after all, was just steps away. But instead the two ladies remained stoic, and seated, throughout the performance. It wasn't until the assailant had leaped from the box to the stage, regained his footing, run across the stage, and then exited the building that Mary verbally responded to the attack. And Clara Harris never responded at all.

Why the curiously delayed reactions from everyone in the

presidential box? And who would plan an escape route that included an exceedingly risky leap onto a very hard stage floor below, especially while wearing riding boots with spurs? One thing that we cannot definitively conclude from the early witness accounts, contrary to popular opinion, is that the guy who hastily exited Ford's Theatre that evening was John Wilkes Booth. In witness accounts recorded years after the official story had cast a long shadow over that day's events, Booth's name pops up fairly often. But it isn't so easy to find in the early accounts. One guy closest to the scene was Army Captain Theodore McGowan, who was seated in Ford's Theatre not far from the entrance to the president's box . . . when called upon to testify at the military tribunal, McGowan had this to say, "I was present at Ford's Theatre on the night of the assassination. I was sitting in the aisle leading by the wall toward the door of the President's box when a man came and disturbed me in my seat, causing me to push my chair forward to permit him to pass; he stopped about three feet from where I was sitting, and leisurely took a survey of the house. I looked at him because he happened to be in my line of sight. . . . I know J. Wilkes Booth, but, not seeing the face of the assassin fully, I did not at the time recognize him as Booth."

So here we have a guy who knew Booth, and yet from just three feet away, with the guy directly in his line of sight, he did not recognize the man in the theater as Booth. It is a fairly safe bet that the government exerted considerable pressure on Captain McGowan to positively identify Booth, and yet he proved unable, or unwilling, to do so. Was it really John Wilkes Booth who entered the presidential box that evening? And whoever it was, did he enter for the purpose of assassinating the president?[2]

H. Donald Winkler writes in *Lincoln and Booth* about the plentiful opportunities Lincoln provided for would-be public assassins given that the president acted like a man who hadn't received more than ten thousand death threats since first entering office.

Fig. 9.5. President Lincoln visits Gen. George McClellan
at Antietam, Maryland, October 1862

The president had made himself an easy target. He stole away
for solitary walks, especially at night. He held public receptions
where security was almost nonexistent. He conferred with generals
in the field. He stood atop a parapet at Fort Stevens on the outskirts of Washington for a clear view of Jubal Early's approaching

Confederate forces as soldiers around him were shot dead. He attended the theater frequently. He had walked virtually unguarded through the streets of the fallen Confederate capital. When he and his family stayed at his summer retreat at the Soldiers' Home on the outskirts of Washington, he often rode back and forth to the White House in an unguarded carriage. Nearly every night, before going to bed, he strolled without protection down a densely shaded path through the White House grounds to the War Department's telegraph office to learn the latest news from the war front.[3]

If indeed Mary Lincoln had killed her husband she had gotten away with it perfectly. More evidence that she was complicit in her husband's murder was the rumor that she had spent the equivalent of twenty-five thousand dollars on mourning dresses a couple of weeks before the assassination. It's also claimed that their son Robert Todd Lincoln knew about his father's affairs, half-sisters, and his mother's drug-fueled, murdering ways but kept his silence and covered up the plot, destroying evidence in order to maintain a cushy job as president of Pullman Railroad. The Rothschilds of course owned that railroad company and made sure Robert Todd remained fat, rich, happy, and totally silent to his grave.

In a bit of weird karma, Robert Todd's life was saved from certain early death by John Wilkes Booth's older brother Edwin, who was also a famous actor.

During the Civil War, a young Robert Todd Lincoln was traveling by train from New York to Washington during a break from his studies at Harvard. He hopped off the train during a stop at Jersey City, only to find himself on an extremely crowded platform. To be polite, Lincoln stepped back to wait his turn to walk across the platform, his back pressed to one of the train's cars. This situation probably seemed harmless enough until the train started moving, which whipped Lincoln around and dropped him into the space between

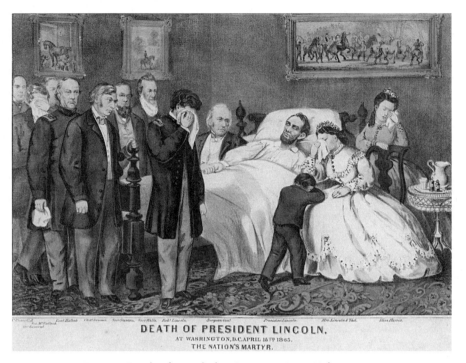

DEATH OF PRESIDENT LINCOLN.
AT WASHINGTON, D.C.APRIL 15ᵀᴴ 1865.
THE NATION'S MARTYR.

Fig. 9.6. Death of Lincoln by Currier & Ives. Nyhistory.org

the platform and train, an incredibly dangerous place to be. Lincoln probably would have been dead meat if a stranger hadn't yanked him out of the hole by his collar. That stranger? None other than Edwin Booth.[4]

While interesting, the theories about Mary being Abraham's killer seem too farfetched to believe, as does the tale of a Booth look-alike meaning to take the fall for the famous actor, even though it's good to remember that there is typically a patsy involved somewhere in conspiracies like this one. As for the twenty-six-year-old John Wilkes Booth, despite already being a major star, he was about to be more famous than he'd ever been. During the time of Lincoln's murder Booth was already extremely rich and famous, the George Clooney of his day. However, his murder of the president makes no sense. What also does not make sense is the fact that he chose not to disguise himself in the act. Remember, he was a superstar actor who had access to disguises and wigs; he could have dressed as anyone he wanted to. Booth practically lived at Ford's Theatre; he even had his mail delivered there. He could have changed into any outfit at any time, and nobody would have noticed that or thought it strange.

However, he was now on the run with a broken leg after having shot the president. But his escape out of town couldn't have gone better. Despite there being a curfew imposed by the War Department, and despite the fact that the Navy Yard Bridge was closed, Booth was allowed to pass over the bridge into Maryland, even though the armed guards were under orders not to let anyone cross. Even stranger is that Booth identified himself to the guards as Booth even though there was no real reason to do so. He even left a bread-crumb trail of business cards with his name on them at different locations throughout the day of the assassination.

A few minutes after Booth had passed into Maryland, David Herold, one of Booth's accomplices, approached the bridge to Maryland, and he too was allowed to pass on by. The guards who let these two conspirators pass were never reprimanded for disobeying orders or punished for letting the president's killer escape from Washington.

Secretary of War Edwin Stanton, who quickly assumed control of the manhunt, had an impressive array of manpower at his disposal: federal troops, metro police, cavalry troops, provost marshals, and Lafayette Baker's NDP detectives. Manpower was deployed first to the north and northwest, the least likely escape routes. The only hole in the dragnet throughout the entire night was the underground route to the South across the Navy Yard Bridge, which was never mentioned that night in any War Department dispatches. Had anyone involved in the manhunt—anyone at all—bothered to stop by the Navy Yard Bridge, it would have been quickly discovered that Booth and a likely accomplice had crossed over into Maryland. But that didn't happen, and pursuers were instead sent on wild goose chases throughout the night.

Another less obvious question is why was Booth so woefully unprepared for his escape? He had to assume that he was going to have to hide out for a time and/or survive on the trail. Why then did he bring no provisions with him? No change of clothes, no bed-roll or blanket, no weapons other than his dagger, no toiletries or razor, no food, nothing that would be required for survival on the road. And the same was true of Herold. Why would Booth, or any reasonably sane person, plot an assassination at a venue from which escape was highly unlikely? Why would the very first phase of that escape involve an incredibly risky leap onto a hard stage floor while wearing riding boots with spurs? Why would his escape route necessitate crossing a bridge where he had no reasonable expectation of being allowed to cross? And why would he have failed to bring along any provisions to survive during his time on the lam?

There is also the question of why there was a two- to three-hour interruption in telegraph service in and out of Washington following the assassination. Stanton had been installed as Secretary of War in January 1862 on the recommendation of Secretary of State William Seward. On February 14, Lincoln had signed Executive Order #1, giving Stanton the power of arbitrary arrest. That too had been at Seward's urging. By early March, Stanton had assumed control of all the nation's telegraph lines and had the machinery comprising the hub of the system moved to the War Department offices. He would soon seize control of the country's transportation system as well. In addition to the civilian telegraph system, the War Department had its own system as well, to transmit secure news and updates on the war effort. Both systems were housed next to Stanton's office at the War Department. On the night of April 14 the civilian telegraph service was out for up to three hours following the assassination, disrupting communications in and out of Washington. That curious fact was never publicly acknowledged.

There was also an unexplained delay in getting the news out on the War Department's telegraph service. The first dispatch concerning the shooting of Lincoln was not written until 1:30 a.m., more than three hours after the events at Ford's Theatre; it wasn't sent until 2:15 a.m., some four hours after the curtain fell at Ford's. Then there were the curious actions of L. A. Gobright, the Associated Press agent in the nation's capital. At around 11:00 p.m., he sent out his first dispatch, which was oddly vague and lacking in details. Even odder, he quickly followed it with a second dispatch instructing recipients that the first message was "stopped." Gobright, it should be noted, was very close to the scene and knew what had gone down. He supposedly rushed over to Ford's immediately after the shooting and is credited with being the guy who allegedly found the derringer on the floor of the box, where it had conveniently been left behind but had apparently not been noticed by anyone else.[5]

Another bizarre bit of the Lincoln assassination conspiracy is how it was possible that in at least six different states (Minnesota, New Hampshire, New York, Ohio, Virginia, and Kentucky) the news of Lincoln's assassination was reported hours before Lincoln and his party had arrived at Ford's Theatre. (It's about as suspicious as the nation's telegraph service going down immediately after the assassination, or the BBC reporting that Building 7 of the World Trade Center fell fifteen minutes before it happened.)

After passing over the bridge and into Maryland, Booth and Herold stopped around midnight at Mary Surratt's tavern in Surrattsville where they were armed with carbines, field glasses, and booze. Afterward, with his leg in bad shape, Booth naturally made a pit stop at a doctor's house. Dr. Samuel Mudd reset Booth's leg and sent him on his way.

Mudd was later thrown in prison in Key West for helping Booth but was later pardoned when it was determined there was no way he could have known that Booth had just shot Lincoln. Mudd, however, was also a slave owner and Southern sympathizer who had met Booth at least three times previously, so it's a bit strange that Mudd is on record as having stated that he didn't recognize the man with the broken leg.

Mudd gave Booth a pair of crutches and was paid twenty-five dollars for his services. After a twelve-hour rest at Dr. Mudd's, Booth and his partner in crime, David Herold, rode on through the Maryland swamps looking for help in crossing the Potomac River. They ditched their horses and then spent five uncomfortable nights hiding in a muggy pine thicket where they not only had to be silent but couldn't light a fire to keep warm at night. All this time Booth was thought to be in painful agony with a broken leg. He was also dirty and wet. This was a situation far removed from the lavish and wealthy lifestyle the famed actor was accustomed to.

What's more astonishing is that it had been ten days since the assassination, and the duo had barely made it out of the Washington area. After five stinky days hiding out in the sticky, cold, Maryland swamps they eventually stole a boat and began to cross the river at night without lights, a daunting task that left them on the east side of the river near where they first started. They made another attempt, crossed over the river into Virginia, and after a few more nights in the woods eventually strode into Richard H. Garrett's tobacco farm, where Booth and his traveling companion would soon ride into the history books. Herold would ride in to surrender and capture and would boast about being part of the crew that killed Lincoln—up until a noose snapped his neck in two during a public hanging. The actor known as John Wilkes Booth would ride to the top of the pop culture conspiracy pantheon.

But who was this charismatic riddle named John Wilkes Booth? Just about everybody knows that he was one of the finest actors of his generation. But do they also know that the Booth family had long been members of the elite in both America and London? Their roots stretched back to at least the early 1700s when their namesake and most famous ancestor, the British John Wilkes, served as a member of Parliament, a judge, a journalist, and eventually mayor of London. Wilkes loved to party with the Rothschilds and was even a member of their secret Hellfire Club, which met in a set of underground caves in London. These caves and hidden rooms were allegedly adorned with bizarre altars where debauched sex games for the elite were known to take place. Here also it is said that child sacrifices and satanic rituals were performed by rich and powerful men, far removed from the eyes of the British public. It's worth wondering if Wilkes ever participated in any raucous Hellfire activities with fellow Hellfire member and founding father Benjamin Franklin. Oddly enough, in 1998, when excavations began on Franklin's elegant four-story Georgian home in London, the basement yielded the remains of at least twelve bodies, six of them children.

The Hellfire Club coined the phrase "Do what thou wilt," which was later made famous by the English occultist Aleister Crowley and is now used and kept relevant by one of the world's most famous rappers Jay-Z. John Wilkes the elder was a member of this elite underground club. And despite being known as the ugliest man in England, he still managed to socialize all night, participating in occult rituals and drunken orgies and never lacking attractive female companions. Although he had been married briefly, Wilkes remained a swinging bachelor for most of his seventy-two years on Earth and fathered a bunch of bastard children. Despite his subpar looks Wilkes had a fat wallet and a gift for "casting a spell" over women. His descendant John Wilkes Booth would also inherent this gift, which was enhanced by a handsome face and great hair.

Booth's other famous ancestors included Henry Booth, the first Earl of Warrington, who lived in the late 1600s, and the earl's son George Booth, who died in 1758 as the last Earl of Warrington. Henry Booth was also a former member of Parliament, respected writer, and a mayor of Chester. Another one of John Wilkes Booth's descendants was Barton Booth, who died in 1733 but not before being hailed as English royalty's most popular actor.

Many generations later, namesake Sydney Barton Booth, a son of Junius Brutus Booth, Jr., would become an actor and writer of some renown before passing away in 1937. The alleged assassin's grandfa-

Fig. 9.7. John Wilkes, the British ancestor of John Wilkes Booth, after Richard Houston (1768). National Portrait Gallery, London

ther was Richard Booth, an eccentric English barrister with a fondness for alcohol—a fondness that would be shared by his son, Junius Brutus Booth, and his grandson, John Wilkes Booth. Junius was born in London in 1796 and was performing on stage by the age of seventeen. . . .

In June 1821, at the age of twenty-five, Junius set sail for America with his mistress, Mary Ann Holmes, leaving behind his wife and only surviving child, Richard Junius Booth. Junius and Mary Ann would pose as man and wife for the next thirty years, producing no fewer than ten illegitimate offspring, four of whom didn't make it through childhood. The pair weren't actually married until 1851, the year Junius finally divorced his actual wife, and were married just one year before Junius passed away in November 1852. Junius was named after one of the notorious assassin ever and set an example for his son by sending letters to Andrew Jackson threatening to slit his throat and have him burned at stake; he even signed the letter and included a return address, nevertheless Jackson dismissed it as a cruel joke or a hoax.

Junius and Mary Ann purchased a 150-acre estate in Maryland that would ultimately feature a large pool, stables, and a Gothic home known as Tudor Hall, listed in the National Register of Historic Places. Junius began construction on the home shortly before his death and so never lived there, though his offspring, including John Wilkes Booth, did. . . . John Wilkes Booth, the ninth of Junius and Mary Ann's ten offspring, was born on May 10, 1838. A well-educated young man, he was regarded as an excellent horseman and marksman as well as a talented athlete. Like his father, he made his acting debut at seventeen, in an 1855 production of *Richard III*. By 1861, he was one of the most popular actors in America, and there was considerable demand for his services. On December 2, 1859, John Wilkes Booth was among the soldiers standing guard on the scaffold when probable agent provocateur John Brown was hanged.

Booth was not a soldier though—he purportedly either borrowed or stole a militia uniform and posed as a soldier to secure the position. On March 4, 1865, Booth found himself prominently placed among the onlookers at Lincoln's second inaugural address. He was there as a guest of U.S. Senator John P. Hale. Unknown at the time was that Booth was secretly engaged to Hale's daughter, Lucy Hale. Senator Hale had worked closely with fellow senator William Seward before Seward's appointment as Secretary of State. Notably, Hale was a northern senator, representing New Hampshire, and he was known for his staunchly abolitionist views. It makes perfect sense then that his daughter would be engaged to an alleged Confederate operative . . . in the aftermath of the Lincoln assassination, actors were viewed with considerable suspicion across the country. The entire cast of *Our American Cousin* was arrested and numerous other productions closed for a time due to the lynch-mob mentality that was sweeping the nation. No one was above suspicion and, as previously noted, more than 2,000 people were arrested as possible co-conspirators. Those with only the loosest connections to the accused coup plotters were scooped up and held for varying lengths of time.

Two of John Wilkes Booth's brothers, Edwin and Junius Brutus, Jr., were fellow actors. Clearly then they had two big strikes against them, which should have put them at the very top of the government's round-up list. And yet not a single member of the Booth clan was arrested in the frenzy of arrests and accusations. Not one. It always helps to have friends in high places.[6]

This is a pretty illustrious pedigree for a man on the run from the law. John Wilkes Booth, injured leg and all, was—together with his coconspirator David Herold—on the lam and eluding capture. Booth had shaved his famous mustache and dyed his jet-black hair a lighter shade of auburn before shacking up in a tobacco barn in Virginia. Here he and Herold hid out while a bounty of one hundred thousand dollars was put on their heads; an enormous sum of money at the time. As Wanted posters were spread around the capital area more than two thousand troops were on the move, looking for Booth and his coconspirator.

The dogs heard it first, rising from the southwest. Distant sounds, yet inaudible to human ears, of metal touching metal; of a hundred hoofs sending vibrations through the earth; of labored breathing from tired horses; of faint human voices. These early warning signs alerted the dogs sleeping under the Garretts' front porch. At the farm, John Garrett, corn-house sentinel, was already awake and the first to hear their approach.

William Garrett, lying on a blanket a few feet from his brother, heard them too. It was after midnight and dark and still inside the farmhouse. Old Richard Garrett and the rest of his family had gone to bed hours ago. All was quiet, too, in the tobacco barn, where John Wilkes Booth and his co-conspirator David Herold were sleeping. The barking dogs and the clanking, rumbling sound finally woke Booth. Recognizing the unique music of cavalry on the move, the assassin knew he had only a minute or two to react.

Booth woke Herold. They snatched up their weapons and rushed to the front of the barn. "We went right up to the barn door and tried to get out," Herold would recall, "but found it was locked." The Garretts—suspecting the fugitives might steal horses—had imprisoned them! Booth wasted no time trying to pry the lock from its mountings. They had to flee the barn before Union troops surrounded it. . . . Finally, at the climax of a 12-day manhunt that had gripped the nation, a heavily armed patrol of 16th New York Cavalry had cornered Lincoln's assassin at the Garrett farm in Port Royal, Virginia. . . . The assassin was surrounded and outnumbered 29 to one. Escape seemed impossible. But then, so had escape from an audience of more than a thousand people at Ford's Theatre. . . . Conger and Baker wanted to burn the barn. The flames and choking smoke would do the job for them, at no risk to the troops. . . . Within minutes an entire corner of the barn was blazing brightly.

The fire illuminated the yard with a yellow-orange glow that flickered eerily across the faces of the men of the 16th. Booth could see them clearly now but held his fire. As the fire gathered momentum, it also lit the inside of the barn so that now, for the first time, the soldiers could see their quarry in the gaps between the slats. Booth had three choices: stay in the barn and burn alive; raise a pistol barrel to his head and blow out his brains; or script his own blaze of glory by hobbling out the front door and doing battle with the manhunters. He would not stay in the barn. And suicide? Never.

He moved to the center of the barn, swiveled his head in every direction, measuring how quickly the flames were engulfing him.

He glanced toward the door and hopped forward, a crutch under his left arm and the carbine in his right, the butt plate against his hip. . . . Sergeant Corbett watched Booth's every move. Corbett had, by stealth, peeked between one of the gaps between the barn's vertical boards. Booth "turn[ed] toward the fire, either to put the fire out, or else to shoot the one who started it, I do not know which; but he was then coming right toward me . . . a little to my right—a full breast view." Now Booth was within easy range of Corbett's pistol. But the sergeant held his fire, "I could have shot him . . . but as long as he was there, making no demonstration to hurt anyone, I did not shoot."

Corbett poked the barrel of his revolver through the slit in the wall and aimed it. The sergeant described what happened next, "Finding the fire gaining upon him, [Booth] turned to the other side of the barn and got toward where the door was; and, as he got there, I saw him make a movement toward the floor. I supposed he was going to fight his way out. One of the men who was watching told me that [Booth] aimed his carbine at him. He was taking aim with the carbine, but at whom I could not say. My mind was upon him attentively to see that he did no harm; and, when I became impressed that it was time, I shot him." Instantly Booth dropped the carbine and crumpled to his knees. He could not rise. He could not lift his arms. He could not move at all.

Like sprinters cued by a starting gun, Baker rushed into the barn with Conger at his heels. Baker caught Booth before he toppled over, and Conger seized the assassin's pistol, having to pry it out of the actor's grasp. "It is Booth, certainly," Conger cried jubilantly. . . . They carried Booth under the locust trees a few yards from the door and laid him on the grass.[7]

This would be Booth's final act. Just a half hour earlier, around three o'clock in the morning on April 26, a group of soldiers surrounded the tobacco barn where Booth and Herold were hiding on the Garrett

Fig. 9.8. The capture and death of John Wilkes Booth near Port Royal,
Virginia, on April 26, 1865. Joseph Williams,
Archives and Special Collections, Dickinson College

Fig. 9.9. The ruins of Garrett's barn where John Wilkes Booth was shot.
Harper's Weekly, 1865

farm, near Port Royal in Virginia. They were surrounded, outgunned,
outnumbered, and ordered to surrender peacefully. The plan was to
take Booth alive. Upon realizing the dreadful situation, Herold surrendered and walked out of the barn with his hands up while Lieutenant

Edward Doherty decided to smoke out Booth by setting the barn on fire. Herold was apprehended as the troops moved inside the barn looking to take Booth alive, but a startled sergeant shot a man who was hiding inside the burning barn.

A few soldiers dragged the body presumed to be that of Booth from the blazing inferno and displayed it to Herold and the rest of platoon. But was it really John Wilkes Booth? Herold didn't think so, declaring that the body was that of a man named Boyd. Who was Boyd? Another Booth look-alike patsy? Did the real Booth escape into the night? Historian Nate Orlowek thinks so. "There is tremendous physical evidence that proved beyond a doubt that John Wilkes Booth, in reality, was not killed by the Federal Government Officers as they claimed. In fact, he lived until January 13, 1903, when he died in Enid, Oklahoma territory."[8]

What? Did the Union soldiers turn in the dead body of Booth's patsy and claim it was Booth's? It would have served them well to have done so considering the large amount of reward money they would get for turning Booth in dead or alive. The sum, per person, would amount to roughly ten thousand dollars each, a life-changing amount of money in those days. It's not hard to find a cover-up in the death of Booth, especially when the evidence pertaining to his "death" was basically nonexistent. This is a view shared by John Shumaker, the army's general counsel to the Department of the Army, who said, "The evidence put forth by the government to support the conclusion that the body was that of John Wilkes Booth was so insubstantial that it would not stand up in a court of law."[9]

Dr. Arthur Chitty, who spent years independently studying the Lincoln assassination, said, "The most persuasive evidence to me, at Garrett's Barn, that the man in the barn was not Booth is the fact that his friend David E. Herold came out of the barn and the first thing he said was, 'The man in there is not Booth.'"[10] Other eyewitnesses also refuted the government's claim that Booth was killed at Garrett's farm. Mrs. Helen Allan, a wife of one of Lincoln's secret service members, told

THE MURDERERS DOOM. MISERABLE DEATH OF J. WILKES BOOTH, THE ASSASSIN OF PRESIDENT LINCOLN.
Shot through the head by Sergeant Boston Corbett in a barn on Garrett's Farm, near Port Royal, near the Rappahannock, April 25, 1865.

Fig. 9.10. John Wilkes Booth getting shot. *Harper's Weekly,* 1865

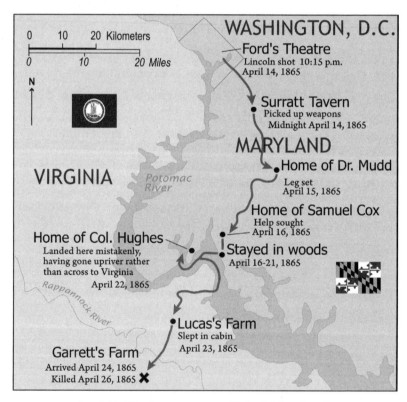

Fig. 9.11. The escape route of John Wilkes Booth
after the assassination of Abraham Lincoln

a journalist that the man her husband saw killed at Garrett's farm had red hair and that the government knew the man was not Booth but was determined to blame Booth anyways.[11]

Booth's jet-black hair was well documented, and even if he had dyed it and shaved his mustache his bearded stubble wouldn't grow back reddish. Eyewitness testimony refuting the official story came from two other Union soldiers—Joseph Zisgen and Wilson Kenzie. Both claimed to have been friends with Booth. In 1922 in a sworn affidavit seventy-seven-year-old Kenzie recalled what he had witnessed at Garrett's farm. "As I rode up, Joe Zisgen called, 'Here, come here Sergeant, this ain't John Wilkes Booth at all.' I could see the color of his hair. I knew at once it wasn't he. His body was exposed and he had no injured leg."[12] Both Kenzie and Zisgen were ordered to keep their mouths shut and were told that dire consequences would befall them if they dared tell the truth. Besides, why would they risk their lives when both men had been offered a decent amount of reward money for having captured the president's killer?

As regards an autopsy, a government doctor who had previously removed a tumor from Booth's neck—someone who was familiar with the actor—performed the autopsy. The doctor was pressured into lying about the body. His report, which had been sealed for seventy years, made it clear that he wasn't so positive that the body was indeed Booth's.

John Frederick May wanted to tell the truth, and he recognized that this was not Booth, but it was made pretty clear to him very early on that "this better be Booth." And so we have the curious affidavit which starts out saying "I'm sure this is Booth." And then goes on to say, "But it doesn't look like Booth. But this is certainly Booth." Signed, John Frederick May. Now, had the government really believed that that body was Booth's, they would have taken pictures of it, they would have had many, many, hundreds of people identify it, but the war department didn't do that. The government knew that that man was not Booth.[13]

In any event, Booth's body was secretly and quickly buried in an unmarked grave near the basement of the Old Naval Prison in Washington. No photographs ever emerged of the corpse.

If John Wilkes Booth wasn't killed at Garrett's farm, then who was? Historians of alternative theories claim that the patsy assigned to take the fall for Booth was the Union double agent James Boyd. Boyd was brought in to replace Booth, who changed outfits and rode off into the night, leaving Herold and Boyd behind at the tobacco barn. Boyd was even the man claimed by Herold that was shot and dragged out of the burning barn instead of Booth. But the government didn't want to hear any of that and moved quickly to close the books on the Lincoln assassination.

Less than twenty-four hours after the killing of "Booth," the trial of his coconspirators resulted in four deaths by hanging (including the first woman ever hanged) and three life sentences in prison. The shady details of the Booth conspiracy were classified top secret and hidden away from the public for more than seven decades.

A bit of background on Boyd: he was a former Confederate agent, having been a stooge for Lincoln's secretary of war, Edwin Stanton, and the War Department. The problem was that Stanton, like Booth, was a fellow Mason and alleged member of the Knights of the Golden Circle. And despite General Lee's surrender just five days prior to Lincoln's assassination, the country was still in turmoil. Confederate president Jefferson Davis had vacated Richmond with all of the gold reserves and ammunition he could carry. He vowed to fight on and, while the nation mourned the loss of their leader, Stanton was under considerable pressure to bring the killer to justice.

However, being that Booth was one of the boys, so to speak, Stanton used Boyd as a patsy to take the place of Booth, thus closing the case and resolving the matter of the president's assassination rather quickly. An old photograph of Boyd proves the striking resemblance to Booth, apart from the reddish hair and auburn mustache. John P. Simonton, who served as a judge advocate for the War Department for more than forty years, claimed, "I studied the evidence in this case and found no definite proof that John Wilkes Booth was ever captured."[14]

Furthermore, during Booth's lifetime nobody had ever claimed that Booth had any tattoos; however, Boyd had his initials, JWB, tattooed on his left hand, a marking duly noted during the autopsy. It's a pretty strange coincidence that Boyd and Booth shared the same initials, and one that wasn't overlooked by Stanton when he chose Boyd as the fall guy for Booth. None of Booth's friends were ever called to the medical inquest to identify his body, despite the fact that Booth was one of the most famous men in America! Andrew and Luther Potter were brothers and famous detectives who had been on Booth's trail from the beginning. When they were summoned to view the corpse, however, one of them commented, "He sure grew a moustache in a hurry. Red, too."

All of the twenty-six detectives who worked on the case and the actual cavalry unit that captured Booth received a good chunk of money after agreeing to sign hush papers claiming that the case was solved and that as such they had no further interest in it. With Boyd killed as the patsy it's claimed that Booth escaped to Texas where he lived under the alias John St. Helen for another thirty-eight years. He was basically on the pension payroll of the Knights of the Golden Circle (KGC), who supported him as long as he kept his mouth shut. But Booth the actor yearned for recognition and was becoming a loudmouth old drunk who consistently blabbed about killing Lincoln.

Now calling himself D. E. George, Booth was on the run from the KGC and living it up in Enid, Oklahoma, as a washed-up drunk yearning to return to the stage and his glory days. Booth's inability to stop blabbing and his sudden disappearance annoyed KGC ringleader and legendary outlaw Jesse James to the point of him finally taking action to silence Booth once and for all. James and fellow KGC members tracked Booth to Oklahoma, where they followed hot on his trail.

But wasn't Jesse James supposed to be dead already? What was he doing in Oklahoma in 1903? According to conspiracy folklore, James had faked his own death in 1882 and continued to live a long life away from the peering eyes of the government. According to *Jesse James Was One of His Names,* the most controversial biography ever written about the outlaw folk hero, James poisoned Booth in cold blood at a hotel tavern in Enid. The book, published in 1975 and written by Del Schrader and James's grandson Jesse James III, has become highly collectible. It's also extremely rare and will cost you upward of a thousand dollars if you're lucky enough to find a copy. It contains so many stories and controversial claims that it's almost hard to take seriously. One of the extreme tales told in the book pertains to the killing of John Wilkes Booth by Jesse James.

According to the book, Booth had been surrounded by KGC agents who were guarding the downstairs area of the hotel. He hadn't been feeling too well that morning and spent most of the day in bed, which is where James and Booth bounty hunter Wild Bill Lincoln (a distant cousin of Abe's) found him when they snuck into his room for a friendly afternoon chat. Booth got up to greet his visitors; however, James wasn't intent on the chat lasting too long as he made the move to kill the unsuspecting Booth instead.

> Jesse went over to the wash stand with a jar of lemonade. Hastily, he pulled two bottles from his pocket and poured pure arsenic into the jar. Then he stirred the mixture with a table fork. He poured the loaded lemonade into a glass. Approaching the bed, Jesse said, "Now, Mr. Booth, I think you've had enough alcohol for tonight. This lemonade will really fix you up. I personally guarantee it." Booth gasped, went into almost a stage fall, but hit the floor with a thud. Jesse James bent over and felt his heart. "Deader than a mackerel," he said. "Wild Bill, stay here. I'm sending up the four agents in the lobby to go through Booth's luggage. I'll be back in a few minutes." The six men were amazed at the records Booth had kept through the years. After they had finished sorting it,

Jesse said, "You know, men, I'm just glad Booth didn't put all this in that crazy book his lawyer wrote—he could have put a noose around all of our necks!"[15]

Jesse and his men scattered Booth's papers around the corpse for easy identification of the body, taking any damning evidence relating to the KGC and all that was left of Booth's money. Jesse then went downstairs and gave the manager of the hotel a gold coin in exchange for checking in on his sick friend George in the morning. Jesse and the boys rode slyly out of town, and the next morning the hotel clerk discovered Booth's body. He reported it to the press, who had an unexpected field day making the news a nationwide event. The story exploded, and within days thousands of reporters from all over America descended on the tiny town of Enid to report about the supposed death of John Wilkes Booth.

Wild Bill Lincoln later wrote, "Our branch of the Lincoln family was never satisfied with what really happened to Booth, and I spent fourteen years of my life running down the true story. Strangely enough, I learned it from Jesse W. James, head of the Confederate underground. I was present at Booth's real death."[16]

Was D. E. George really the famed actor John Wilkes Booth? To the townsfolk of Enid, whomever he was, he sure was a strange character. He had only been in town for three weeks and claimed to be a house painter yet didn't know how to paint. He didn't have any source of income but always had money, despite being found penniless when he died. He was also a notorious loud-mouthed drunk who loved to frequent the town's taverns, where he drank the night away and astonished the bar patrons with his lengthy recitals of Shakespeare. He was also known to have said many times, "I killed the best man that ever lived," but he never elaborated any further on the statement. Whether George was Booth is debatable, but if he was, he couldn't have asked for a more sensational final act. Because of the apparently suicide-inspired arsenic drinking that Booth committed before he died, his corpse was literally turned into a mummy. Soon this mummified corpse was part of a traveling circus and presented to the mystified public as the mummy of John Wilkes Booth.

Even as a leather-faced dead guy, people still paid good money to see the mummified body of Lincoln's killer. Booth was in demand once again, proving that he was indeed perhaps the greatest actor in American history. Unfortunately Booth's mysterious mummified body vanished from the public eye in the late 1950s. However, before the mummy disappeared into the silent night, six Chicago physicians examined it and noted a scarred right eyebrow, a crushed right thumb, and the notorious broken left leg—all bizarre characteristics that John Wilkes Booth was known to have had.

The only way to really close the case of John Wilkes Booth would be through a forensic cross-examination of Booth's DNA. This could easily be done given that Booth's descendants have agreed to allow the DNA from John Wilke's brother Edwin to be tested alongside the known bits of Booth's body that have survived, like his hand. They're even up for exhuming the rest of Booth's body or the body of whomever it was that was killed at Garrett's farm and ended up being buried in an unmarked grave at Green Mount Cemetery in Baltimore. Some even believe that Edwin killed Lincoln instead of John Wilkes in a case of sibling rivalry. Modernhealthcare.com reports:

> One way to answer the question would require exhuming the body in Baltimore. Booth's descendants—supported by the Smithsonian Institution, which said it thinks the Booth escape theory is worth a closer look—filed a court case to exhume the body, but that request was denied in 1995. The judge's decision cited possibly severe water damage to the plot, evidence that siblings were buried on top of Booth, and the "less than convincing escape/coverup theory." So, how does the National Museum of Health and Medicine fit in?
>
> The Silver Spring, Maryland, museum holds three of Booth's

Fig. 9.12. The alleged mummy of John Wilkes Booth

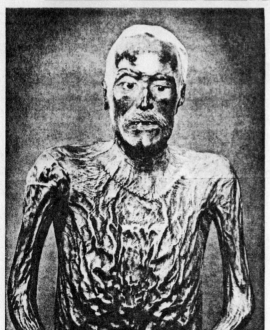

Fig. 9.13. Another image of the mummy purported to be John Wilkes Booth

ALLEGED TO BE mummy of John Wilkes Booth, Lincoln's assassin, this body of an Enid, Okla., "suicide," dead 28 years, was examined in 1931 by a group of distinguished Chicago scientists. Note upraised right eyebrow. This was known to have existed in the living Booth; other similarities led scientists to conclude that this was indeed Booth. Evidently he had escaped, following the assassination.

Fig. 9.14. People paying to see Booth's mummy, circa 1931. William Vandervert, the LIFE Picture Collection, Getty Images

Fig. 9.15. People gathered around the mummy of John Wilkes Booth. William Vandervert, the LIFE Picture Collection, Getty Images

cervical vertebrae, which were kept by the U.S. Army after an autopsy. Given advancements in technology, DNA from the bones of Booth's thespian brother, Edwin, could be compared with DNA from the museum's bones to end the controversy. And a direct descendent has agreed to the exhumation of Edwin Booth, who was buried in Boston. However, earlier this year, the U.S. Army Medical Command, which is in charge of the museum, denied the request, since a proposed DNA test would require using less than 0.4 grams of the bones. In a letter to Rep. Chris Van Hollen (D-Md.), who helped submit the request, the museum said "the need to preserve these bones for future generations compels us to decline the destructive test."[17]

Thus, much like the hero Meriwether Lewis in our first book, *The Suppressed History of America,* Booth joins the ranks of mythical American characters whose past has been conveniently refabricated by the U.S. government in order to present an officially sanctioned version of the truth. There is nothing more to see here, so move along, please. The legacies of Booth and Lewis will therefore continue to be decorated with an asterisk and relegated to the sidelines of history despite the fact that in the age of DNA forensics their cold cases could be solved quite easily once and for all. As the nation mourned the loss of its president 1865 closed unceremoniously, an air of uncertainty hanging over the New Year. The president was dead, the war was over, and Lincoln's experimental currency, the greenback, which had propelled the nation to newfound prosperity, was now worthless. The Rothschilds quickly went on the offensive and basically eradicated Lincoln's entire economic program, making sure that only gold and silver (they owned it all) would once again be considered legal tender.

This period after the Civil War was probably one of the worst times to be alive in America. There was no money, very little work, and expansion west depended primarily on the railroads and the cooperation of the Native Americans. As the 1870s loomed, the Rothschilds were once again slowly gaining control of the American financial system. Other presidents would rise up against them only to be murdered, and those pesky giant bones were still being unearthed.

But those are all tales for part three of our saga about the suppressed history of America.

APPENDIX

President Jackson's Veto Message Regarding the Bank of the United States

July 10, 1832

Andrew Jackson was vehemently opposed to the idea of a central bank in America and in 1832 wrote a letter to Congress and the general public articulating the rationale for his opposition. An initial portion of this letter is found in chapter 4; below is the letter in its entirety.

To the Senate:

The bill "to modify and continue" the act entitled "An act to incorporate the subscribers to the Bank of the United States" was presented to me on the 4th July instant. Having considered it with that solemn regard to the principles of the Constitution which the day was calculated to inspire, and come to the conclusion that it ought not to become a law, I herewith return it to the Senate, in which it originated, with my objections. A bank of the United States is in many respects convenient for the Government and useful to the people. Entertaining this opinion, and deeply impressed with the belief that some of the powers and privileges possessed by the existing bank are unauthorized by the Constitution, subversive of the rights of the States, and dangerous to the liberties of the people, I felt it my duty at an early period of my Administration to call the attention of Congress to the practicability of organizing an institution combining all its advantages and obviating these objections. I sincerely regret that in the act before me I can perceive none of those modifications of the bank charter which are necessary, in my opinion, to make it compatible with justice, with sound policy, or with the Constitution of our country.

The present corporate body, denominated the president, directors, and company of the Bank of the United States, will have existed at the time this act is intended to take effect twenty years. It enjoys an exclusive privilege of banking under the authority of the General Government, a monopoly of its favor and support, and, as a necessary consequence, almost a monopoly of the foreign and domestic exchange. The powers, privileges, and favors bestowed upon it in the original charter, by increasing the value of the stock far above its par value, operated as a gratuity of many millions to the stockholders.

An apology may be found for the failure to guard against this result in the consideration that the effect of the original act of incorporation could not be certainly foreseen at the time of its passage. The act before me proposes another gratuity to the holders of the same stock, and in many cases to the same men, of at least seven millions more. This donation finds no apology in any uncertainty as to the effect of the act. On all hands it is conceded that its passage will increase at least so or 30 percent more the market price of the stock, subject to the payment of the annuity of $200,000 per year secured by the act, thus adding in a moment one-fourth to its par value. It is not our own citizens only who are to receive the bounty of our Government. More than eight million of the stocks of this bank are held by foreigners. By this act the American Republic proposes virtually to make them a present of some millions of dollars. For these gratuities to foreigners and to some of our own opulent citizens the act secures no equivalent whatever. They are the certain gains of the present stockholders under the operation of this act, after making full allowance for the payment of the bonus.

Every monopoly and all exclusive privileges are granted at the expense of the public, which ought to receive a fair equivalent. The many millions which this act proposes to bestow on the stockholders of the existing bank must come directly or indirectly out of the earnings of the American people. It is due to them, therefore, if their Government sells monopolies and exclusive privileges, that they should at least exact for them as much as they are worth in open market. The value of the monopoly in this case may be correctly ascertained. The twenty-eight million of stocks would probably be at an advance of 50 percent, and command in market at least $42,000,000, subject to the payment of the present bonus. The present value of the monopoly, therefore, is $17,000,000, and this act proposes to sell for three millions, payable in fifteen annual installments of $200,000 each.

It is not conceivable how the present stockholders can have any claim to the special favor of the Government. The present corporation has enjoyed its monopoly during the period stipulated in the original contract. If we must have such a corporation, why should not the Government sell out the whole stock and thus secure to the people the full market value of the privileges granted? Why should not Congress create and sell twenty-eight million of stocks, incorporating the purchasers with all the powers and privileges secured in this act and putting the premium upon the sales into the Treasury?

But this act does not permit competition in the purchase of this monopoly. It seems to be predicated on the erroneous idea that the present stockholders have a prescriptive right not only to the favor but to the bounty of Government. It appears that more than a fourth part of the stock is held by foreigners and the residue is held by a few hundred of our own citizens, chiefly of the richest class. For their benefit does this act exclude the whole American people from competition in the purchase of this monopoly and dispose of it for many millions less than it is worth. This seems the less excusable because some of our citizens not now stockholders petitioned that the door of competition might be opened, and offered to take a charter on terms much more favorable to the Government and country. But this proposition, although made by men whose aggregate wealth is believed to be equal to all the private stock in the existing bank, has been set aside, and the bounty of our Government is proposed to be again bestowed on the few who have been fortunate enough to secure the stock and at this moment wield the power of the existing institution. I cannot perceive the justice or policy of this course. If our Government must sell monopolies, it would seem to be its duty to take nothing less than their full value, and if gratuities must be made once in fifteen or twenty years let them not be bestowed on the subjects of a foreign government nor upon a designated and favored class of men in our own country. It is but justice and good policy, as far as the nature of the case will admit, to confine our favors to our own fellow-citizens, and let each in his turn enjoy an opportunity to profit by our bounty. In the bearings of the act before me upon these points I find ample reasons why it should not become a law.

It has been urged as an argument in favor of rechartering the present bank that the calling in its loans will produce great embarrassment and distress. The time allowed to close its concerns is ample, and if it has been well managed its pressure will be light, and heavy only in case its management has been bad. If, therefore, it shall produce distress, the fault will be its own, and it would furnish a reason against renewing a power which has been so obviously abused. But will there ever be a time when this reason will be less powerful? To acknowledge its force is to admit that the bank ought to be perpetual, and as a consequence the present stockholders and those inheriting their rights as successors be established a privileged order, clothed both with great political power and enjoying immense pecuniary advantages from their connection with the Government. The modifications of the existing charter proposed by this act are not such, in my view, as make it consistent with the rights of the States or the liberties of the people. The qualification of the right of the bank to hold real estate, the limitation of its power to establish branches, and the power reserved to Congress to forbid the circulation of small notes are restrictions comparatively of little value or importance. All the objectionable principles of the existing corporation, and most of its odious features, are retained without alleviation.

The fourth section provides "that the notes or bills of the said corporation, although the same be, on the faces thereof, respectively made payable at one place only, shall nevertheless be received by the said corporation at the bank or at any of the offices of discount and deposit thereof if tendered in liquidation or payment of any balance or balances due to said corporation or to such office of discount and deposit from any other incorporated bank." This provision secures to the State banks a legal privilege in the Bank of the United States which is withheld from all private citizens. If a State bank in Philadelphia owe the Bank of the United States and have notes issued by the St. Louis branch, it can pay the debt with those notes, but if a merchant, mechanic, or other private citizen be in like circumstances he cannot by law pay his debt with those notes, but must sell them at a discount or send them to St. Louis to be cashed. This boon conceded to the State banks, though not unjust in itself, is most odious because it does not measure out equal justice to the high and the low, the rich and the poor. To the extent of its practical effect it is a bond of union among the banking establishments of the nation, erecting them into an interest separate from that of the people, and its necessary tendency is to unite the Bank of the United States and the State banks in any measure which may be thought conducive to their common interest.

The ninth section of the act recognizes principles of worse tendency than any provision of the present charter. It enacts that "the cashier of the bank shall annually report to the Secretary of the Treasury the names of all stockholders who are not resident citizens of the United States, and on the application of the treasurer of any State shall make out and transmit to such treasurer a list of stockholders residing in or citizens of such State, with the amount of stock owned by each." Although this provision, taken in connection with a decision of the Supreme Court, surrenders, by its silence, the right of the States to tax the banking institutions created by this corporation under the name of branches throughout the Union, it is evidently intended to be construed as a concession of their right to tax that portion of the stock which may be held by their own citizens and residents. In this light, if the act becomes a law, it will be understood by the States, who will probably proceed to levy a tax equal to that paid upon the stock of banks incorporated by themselves. In some States that tax is now 1 percent, either on the capital or on the shares, and that may be assumed as the amount which all citizen or resident stockholders would be taxed under the operation of this act. As it is only the stock held in the States and not that employed within them which would be subject to taxation, and as the names of foreign stockholders are not to be reported to the treasurers of the States, it is obvious that the stock held by them will be exempt from this burden. Their annual profits will therefore be 1 percent more than the citizen stockholders, and as the annual dividends of the bank may be safely estimated at 7 percent, the stock will be worth 10 or 15 percent more to foreigners than to citizens of the United States. To appreciate the effects which this state of things will produce, we must take a brief review of the operations and present condition of the Bank of the United States.

By documents submitted to Congress at the present session it appears that on the 1st of January, 1832, of the twenty-eight millions of private stock in the corporation, $8,405,500 were held by foreigners, mostly of Great Britain. The amount of stock held in the nine Western and Southwestern States is $140,200, and in the four Southern States is $5,623,100, and in the Middle and Eastern States is about $13,522,000. The profits of the bank in 1831, as shown in a statement to Congress, were about $3,455,598; of this there accrued in the nine western States about $1,640,048; in the four Southern States about $352,507, and in the Middle and Eastern States about $1,463,041. As little stock is held in the West, it is obvious that the debt of the people in that section to the bank is principally a debt to the Eastern and foreign stockholders; that the interest they pay upon it is carried into the Eastern States and into Europe, and that it is a burden upon their industry and a drain of their currency, which no country can bear without inconvenience and occasional distress. To meet this burden and equalize the exchange operations of the bank, the amount of specie drawn from those States through its branches within the last two years, as shown by its official reports, was about $6,000,000. More than half a million of this amount does not stop in the Eastern States, but passes on to Europe to pay the dividends of the foreign stockholders. In the principle of taxation recognized by this act the Western States find no adequate compensation for this perpetual burden on their industry and drain of their currency. The branch bank at Mobile made last year $95,140, yet under the provisions of this act the State of Alabama can raise no revenue from these profitable operations, because not a share of the stock is held by any of her citizens. Mississippi and Missouri are in the same condition in relation to the branches at Natchez and St. Louis, and such, in a greater or less degree, is the condition of every Western State. The tendency of the plan of taxation which this act proposes will be to place the whole United States in the same relation to foreign countries which the Western States now bear to the Eastern. When by a tax on resident stockholders the stock of this bank is made worth 10 or 15 per cent more to foreigners than to residents, most of it will inevitably leave the country. Thus will this provision in its practical effect deprive the Eastern as well as the Southern and Western States of the means of raising a revenue from the extension of business and great profits of this institution. It will make the American people debtors to aliens in nearly the whole amount due to this bank, and send across the Atlantic from two to five millions of specie every year to pay the bank dividends.

In another of its bearings this provision is fraught with danger. Of the twenty-five directors of this bank five are chosen by the Government and twenty by the citizen stockholders. From all voice in these elections the foreign stockholders are excluded by the charter. In proportion, therefore, as the stock is transferred to foreign holders the extent of suffrage in the choice of directors is curtailed. Already is almost a third of the stock in foreign hands and not represented in elections. It is constantly passing out of the country, and this act will accelerate its departure. The entire control of the institution would necessarily fall into the hands of a few citizen stockholders, and the ease with which the object would be accomplished would be a temptation to designing men to secure that control in their own hands by monopolizing the remaining stock. There is danger that a president and directors would then be able to elect themselves from year to year, and without responsibility or control manage the whole concerns of the bank during the existence of its charter. It is easy to conceive that great evils to our country and its institutions millet flow from such a concentration of power in the hands of a few men irresponsible to the people. Is there no danger to our liberty and independence in a bank that in its nature has so little to bind it to our country? The president of the bank has told us that most of the State banks exist by its forbearance. Should its influence become concentered, as it may under the operation of such an act as this, in the hands of a self-elected directory whose interests are identified with those of the foreign stockholders, will there not be cause to tremble for the purity of our elections in peace and for the independence of our country in war? Their power would be great whenever they might choose to exert it; but if this monopoly were regularly renewed every fifteen or twenty years on terms proposed by themselves, they might seldom in peace put forth their strength to influence elections or control the affairs of the nation. But if any private citizen or public functionary should interpose to curtail its powers or prevent a renewal of its privileges, it cannot be doubted that he would be made to feel its influence.

Should the stock of the bank principally pass into the hands of the subjects of a foreign country, and we should unfortunately become involved in a war with that country, what would be our condition? Of the course which would be pursued by a bank almost wholly owned by the subjects of a foreign power, and managed by those whose interests, if not affections, would run in the same direction there can be no doubt. All its operations within would be in aid of the hostile fleets and armies without. Controlling our currency, receiving our public moneys, and holding thousands of our citizens in dependence, it would be more formidable and dangerous than the naval and military power of the enemy. If we must have a bank with private stockholders, every consideration of sound policy and every impulse of American feeling admonishes that it should be purely American. Its stockholders should be composed exclusively of our own citizens, who at least ought to be friendly to our Government and willing to support it in times of difficulty and danger. So abundant is domestic capital that competition in subscribing for the stock of local banks has recently led almost to riots. To a bank exclusively of American stockholders, possessing the powers and privileges granted by this act, subscriptions for $200,000,000 could be readily obtained. Instead of sending abroad the stock of the bank in which the Government must deposit its funds and on which it must rely to sustain its credit in times of emergency, it would rather seem to be expedient to prohibit its sale to aliens under penalty of absolute forfeiture.

It is maintained by the advocates of the bank that its constitutionality in all its features ought to be considered as settled by precedent and by the decision of the Supreme Court. To this conclusion I cannot assent. Mere precedent is a dangerous source of authority, and should not be regarded as deciding questions of constitutional power except where the acquiescence of the people and the States can be considered as well settled. So far from this being the case on this subject, an argument against the bank might be based on precedent. One Congress, in 1791, decided in favor of a bank; another, in 1811, decided against it. One Congress, in 1815, decided against a bank; another, in 1816, decided in its favor. Prior to the present Congress, therefore, the precedents drawn from that source were equal. If we resort to the States, the expressions of legislative, judicial, and executive opinions against the bank have been probably to those in its favor as 4 to 1. There is nothing in precedent, therefore, which, if its authority were admitted, ought to weigh in favor of the act before me.

If the opinion of the Supreme Court covered the whole ground of this act, it ought not to control the coordinate authorities of this Government. The Congress, the Executive, and the Court must each for itself be guided by its own opinion of the Constitution. Each public officer who takes an oath to support the Constitution swears that he will support it as he understands it, and not as it is understood by others. It is as much the duty of the House of Representatives, of the Senate, and of the President to decide upon the constitutionality of any bill or resolution which may be presented to them for passage or approval as it is of the supreme judges when it may be brought before them for judicial decision. The opinion of the judges has no more authority over Congress than the opinion of Congress has over the judges, and on that point the President is independent of both. The authority of the Supreme Court must not, therefore, be permitted to control the Congress or the Executive when acting in their legislative capacities, but to have only such influence as the force of their reasoning may deserve.

But in the case relied upon the Supreme Court have not decided that all the features of this corporation are compatible with the Constitution. It is true that the court have said that the law incorporating the bank is a constitutional exercise of power by Congress; but taking into view the whole opinion of the court and the reasoning by which they have come to that conclusion, I understand them to have decided that inasmuch as a bank is an appropriate means for carrying into effect the enumerated powers of the General Government, therefore the law incorporating it is in accordance with that provision of the Constitution which declares that Congress shall have power "to make all laws which shall be necessary and proper for carrying those powers into execution." Having satisfied themselves that the word necessary in the Constitution means "needful," "requisite," "essential," "conducive to," and that "a bank" is a convenient, a useful, and essential instrument in the prosecution of the Government's "fiscal operations," they conclude that to "use one must be within the discretion of Congress" and that "the act to incorporate the Bank of the United States is a law made in pursuance of the Constitution;" "but," say they, "where the law is not prohibited and is really calculated to effect any of the objects entrusted to the Government, to undertake here to inquire into the degree of its necessity would be to pass the line which circumscribes the judicial department and to tread on legislative ground."

The principle here affirmed is that the degree of its necessity, involving all the details of a banking institution, is a question exclusively for legislative consideration. A bank is constitutional, but it is the province of the Legislature to determine whether this or that particular power, privilege, or exemption is "necessary and proper" to enable the bank to discharge its duties to the Government, and from their decision there is no appeal to the courts of justice. Under the decision of the Supreme Court, therefore, it is the exclusive province of Congress and the President to decide whether the particular features of this act are necessary and proper in order to enable the bank to perform conveniently and efficiently the public duties assigned to it as a fiscal agent, and therefore constitutional, or unnecessary and improper, and therefore unconstitutional.

Without commenting on the general principle affirmed by the Supreme Court, let us examine the details of this act in accordance with the rule of legislative action which they have laid down. It will be found that many of the powers and privileges conferred on it cannot be supposed necessary for the purpose for which it is proposed to be created, and are not, therefore, means necessary to attain the end in view, and consequently not justified by the Constitution. The original act of incorporation, section 2I, enacts "that no other bank shall be established by any future law of the United States during the continuance of the corporation hereby created, for which the faith of the United States is hereby pledged: Provided, Congress may renew existing charters for banks within the District of Columbia not increasing the capital thereof, and may also establish any other bank or banks in said District with capitals not exceeding in the whole $6,000,000 if they shall deem it expedient." This provision is continued in force by the act before me fifteen years from the ad of March, 1836.

If Congress possessed the power to establish one bank, they had power to establish more than one if in their opinion two or more banks had been necessary to facilitate the execution of the powers delegated to them in the Constitution. If they possessed the power to establish a second bank, it was a power derived from the Constitution to be exercised from time to time, and at any time when the interests of the country or the emergencies of the Government might make it expedient. It was possessed by one Congress as well as another, and by all Congresses alike, and alike at every session. But the Congress of 1816, have taken it away from their successors for twenty years, and the Congress of 1832 proposes to abolish it for fifteen years more. It cannot be necessary or proper for Congress to barter away or divest themselves of any of the powers-vested in them by the Constitution to be exercised for the public good. It is not "necessary" to the efficiency of the bank, nor is it proper in relation to themselves and their successors. They may properly use the discretion vested in them, but they may not limit the discretion of their successors. This restriction on themselves and grant of a monopoly to the bank is therefore unconstitutional.

In another point of view this provision is a palpable attempt to amend the Constitution by an act of legislation. The Constitution declares that "the Congress shall have power to exercise exclusive legislation in all cases whatsoever" over the District of Columbia. Its constitutional power, therefore, to establish banks in the District of Columbia and increase their capital at will is unlimited and uncontrollable by any other power than that which gave authority to the Constitution. Yet this act declares that Congress shall not increase the capital of existing banks, nor create other banks with capitals exceeding in the whole $6,000,000. The Constitution declares that Congress shall have power to exercise exclusive legislation over this District in all cases whatsoever, and this act declares they shall not. Which is the supreme law of the land? This provision cannot be necessary or proper or constitutional unless the absurdity be admitted that whenever it be "necessary and proper" in the opinion of Congress they have a right to barter away one portion of the powers vested in them by the Constitution as a means of executing the rest.

On two subjects only does the Constitution recognize in Congress the power to grant exclusive privileges or monopolies. It declares that "Congress shall have power to promote the progress of science and useful arts by securing for limited times to authors and inventors the exclusive right to their respective writings and discoveries." Out of this express delegation of power have grown our laws of patents and copyrights. As the Constitution expressly delegates to Congress the power to grant exclusive privileges in these cases as the means of executing the substantive power "to promote the progress of science and useful arts," it is consistent with the fair rules of construction to conclude that such a power was not intended to be granted as a means of accomplishing any other end. On every other subject which comes within the scope of Congressional power there is an ever-living discretion in the use of proper means, which cannot be restricted or abolished without an amendment of the Constitution. Every act of Congress, therefore, which attempts by grants of monopolies or sale of exclusive privileges for a limited time, or a time without limit, to restrict or extinguish its own discretion in the choice of means to execute its delegated powers is equivalent to a legislative amendment of the Constitution, and palpably unconstitutional. This act authorizes and encourages transfers of its stock to foreigners and grants them an exemption from all State and national taxation. So far from being necessary and proper that the bank should possess this power to make it a safe and efficient agent of the Government in its fiscal operations, it is calculated to convert the Bank of the United States into a foreign bank, to impoverish our people in time of peace, to disseminate a foreign influence through every section of the Republic, and in war to endanger our independence.

The several States reserved the power at the formation of the Constitution to regulate and control titles and transfers of real property, and most, if not all, of them have laws disqualifying aliens from acquiring or holding lands within their limits. But this act, in disregard of the undoubted right of the States to prescribe such disqualifications, gives to aliens stockholders in this bank an interest and title, as members of the corporation, to all the real property it may acquire within any of the States of this Union. This privilege granted to aliens is not necessary to enable the bank to perform its public duties, nor in any sense proper, because it is vitally subversive of the rights of the States.

The Government of the United States has no constitutional power to purchase lands within the States except "for the erection of forts, magazines, arsenals, dockyards, and other needful buildings," and even for these objects only "by the consent of the legislature of the State in which the same shall be." By making themselves stockholders in the bank and granting to the corporation the power to purchase lands for other purposes they assume a power not granted in the Constitution and grant to others what they do not themselves possess. It is not necessary to the receiving, safe-keeping, or transmission of the funds of the Government that the bank should possess this power, and it is not proper that Congress should thus enlarge the powers delegated to them in the Constitution.

The old Bank of the United States possessed a capital of only $11,000,000, which was found fully sufficient to enable it with dispatch and safety to perform all the functions required of it by the Government. The capital of the present bank is $35,000,000— at least twenty-four more than experience has proved to be necessary to enable a bank to perform its public functions. The public debt which existed during the period of the old bank and on the establishment of the new has been nearly paid off, and our revenue will soon be reduced. This increase of capital is therefore not for public but for private purposes. The Government is the only proper judge where its agents should reside and keep their offices, because it best knows where their presence will be necessary. It cannot, therefore, be necessary or proper to authorize the bank to locate branches where it pleases to perform the public service, without consulting the Government, and contrary to its will. The principle laid down by the Supreme Court concedes that Congress cannot establish a bank for purposes of private speculation and gain, but only as a means of executing the delegated powers of the General Government. By the same principle a branch bank cannot constitutionally be established for other than public purposes. The power which this act gives to establish two branches in any State, without the injunction or request of the Government and for other than public purposes, is not necessary to the due execution of the powers delegated to Congress.

The bonus which is exacted from the bank is a confession upon the face of the act that the powers granted by it are greater than are necessary to its character of a fiscal agent. The Government does not tax its officers and agents for the privilege of serving it. The bonus of a million and a half required by the original charter and that of three millions proposed by this act are not exacted for the privilege of giving "the necessary facilities for transferring the public funds from place to place within the United States or the Territories thereof, and for distributing the same in payment of the public creditors without charging commission or claiming allowance on account of the difference of exchange," as required by the act of incorporation, but for something more beneficial to the stockholders. The original act declares that it (the bonus) is granted "in consideration of the exclusive privileges and benefits conferred by this act upon the said bank," and the act before me declares it to be "in consideration of the exclusive benefits and privileges continued by this act to the said corporation for fifteen years, as aforesaid." It is therefore for "exclusive privileges and benefits" conferred for their own use and emolument, and not for the advantage of the

Government, that a bonus is exacted. These surplus powers for which the bank is required to pay cannot surely be necessary to make it the fiscal agent of the Treasury. If they were, the exaction of a bonus for them would not be proper.

It is maintained by some that the bank is a means of executing the constitutional power "to coin money and regulate the value thereof." Congress has established a mint to coin money and passed laws to regulate the value thereof. The money so coined, with its value so regulated, and such foreign coins as Congress may adopt are the only currency known to the Constitution. But if they have other power to regulate the currency, it was conferred to be exercised by themselves, and not to be transferred to a corporation. If the bank be established for that purpose, with a charter unalterable without its consent, Congress has parted with its power for a term of years, during which the Constitution is a dead letter. It is neither necessary nor proper to transfer its legislative power to such a bank, and therefore unconstitutional. By its silence, considered in connection with the decision of the Supreme Court in the case of McCulloch against the State of Maryland, this act takes from the States the power to tax a portion of the banking business carried on within their limits, in subversion of one of the strongest barriers which secured them against Federal encroachments. Banking, like farming, manufacturing, or any other occupation or profession, is a business, the right to follow which is not originally derived from the laws. Every citizen and every company of citizens in all of our States possessed the right until the State legislatures deemed it good policy to prohibit private banking by law. If the prohibitory State laws were now repealed, every citizen would again possess the right. The State banks are a qualified restoration of the right which has been taken away by the laws against banking, guarded by such provisions and limitations as in the opinion of the State legislatures the public interest requires. These corporations, unless there be an exemption in their charter, are, like private bankers and banking companies, subject to State taxation. The manner in which these taxes shall be laid depends wholly on legislative discretion. It may be upon the bank, upon the stock, upon the profits, or in any other mode which the sovereign power shall will.

Upon the formation of the Constitution the States guarded their taxing power with peculiar jealousy. They surrendered it only as it regards imports and exports. In relation to every other object within their jurisdiction, whether persons, property, business, or professions, it was secured in as ample a manner as it was before possessed. All persons, though United States officers, are liable to a poll tax by the States within which they reside. The lands of the United States are liable to the usual land tax, except in the new States, from whom agreements that they will not tax unsold lands are exacted when they are admitted into the Union. Horses, wagons, any beasts or vehicles, tools, or property belonging to private citizens, though employed in the service of the United States, are subject to State taxation. Every private business, whether carried on by an officer of the General Government or not, whether it be mixed with public concerns or not, even if it be carried on by the Government of the United States itself, separately or in partnership, falls within the scope of the taxing power of the State. Nothing comes more fully within it than banks and the business of banking, by whomsoever instituted and carried on. Over this whole subject-matter it is just as absolute, unlimited, and uncontrollable as if the Constitution had never been adopted, because in the formation of that instrument it was reserved without qualification.

The principle is conceded that the States cannot rightfully tax the operations of the General Government. They cannot tax the money of the Government deposited in the State banks, nor the agency of those banks in remitting it; but will any man maintain that their mere selection to perform this public service for the General Government would exempt the State banks and their ordinary business from State taxation? Had the United States, instead of establishing a bank at Philadelphia, employed a private banker to keep and transmit their funds, would it have deprived Pennsylvania of the right to tax his bank and his usual banking operations? It will not be pretended. Upon what principal, then, are the banking establishments of the Bank of the United States and their usual banking operations to be exempted from taxation? It is not their public agency or the deposits of the Government which the States claim a right to tax, but their banks and their banking powers, instituted and exercised within State jurisdiction for their private emolument those powers and privileges for which they pay a bonus, and which the states' tax in their own banks. The exercise of these powers within a State, no matter by whom or under what authority, whether by private citizens in their original right, by corporate bodies created by the States, by foreigners or the agents of foreign governments located within their limits, forms a legitimate object of State taxation. From this and like sources, from the persons, property, and business that are found residing, located, or carried on under their jurisdiction, must the States, since the surrender of their right to raise a revenue from imports and exports, draw all the money necessary for the support of their governments and the maintenance of their independence. There is no more appropriate subject of taxation than banks, banking, and bank stocks, and none to which the States ought more pertinaciously to cling. It cannot be necessary to the character of the bank as a fiscal agent of the Government that its private business should be exempted from that taxation to which all the State banks are liable, nor can I conceive it proper that the substantive and most essential powers reserved by the States shall be thus attacked and annihilated as a means of executing the powers delegated to the General Government. It may be safely assumed that none of those sages who had an agency in forming or adopting our Constitution ever imagined that any portion of the taxing power of the States not prohibited to them nor delegated to Congress was to be swept away and annihilated as a means of executing certain powers delegated to Congress.

If our power over means is so absolute that the Supreme Court will not call in question the constitutionality of an act of Congress the subject of which "is not prohibited, and is really calculated to effect any of the objects entrusted to the Government," although, as in the case before me, it takes away powers expressly granted to Congress and rights scrupulously reserved to the States, it becomes us to proceed in our legislation with the utmost caution. Though not directly, our own powers and the rights of the States may be indirectly legislated away in the use of means to execute substantive powers. We may not enact that Congress shall not have the power of exclusive legislation over the District of Columbia, but we may pledge the faith of the United States that as a means of executing other powers it shall not be exercised for twenty years or forever. We may not pass an act prohibiting the States to tax the banking business carried on within their limits, but we may, as a means of executing our powers over other objects, place that business in the hands of our agents and then declare it exempt from State taxation in their hands. Thus may our own powers and the rights of the States, which we cannot directly curtail or invade, be frittered away and extinguished in the use of means employed by us to execute other powers. That a bank of the United States, competent to all the duties which may be required by the Government, might be so organized as not to infringe on our own delegated powers or the reserved rights of the States I do not entertain a doubt. Had the Executive been called upon to furnish the project of such an institution, the duty would have been cheerfully performed. In the absence of such a call it was obviously proper that he should confine himself to pointing out those prominent features in the act presented which in his opinion make it incompatible with the Constitution and sound policy. A general discussion will now take place, eliciting new light and settling important principles; and a new Congress, elected in the midst of such discussion, and furnishing an equal representation of the people according to the last census, will bear to the Capitol the verdict of public opinion, and, I doubt not, bring this important question to a satisfactory result.

Under such circumstances the bank comes forward and asks a renewal of its charter for a term of fifteen years upon conditions which not only operate as a gratuity to the stockholders of many millions of dollars, but will sanction any abuses and legalize any encroachments. Suspicions are entertained and charges are made of gross abuse and violation of its charter. An investigation unwillingly conceded and so restricted in time as necessarily to make it incomplete and unsatisfactory discloses enough to excite suspicion and alarm. In the practices of the principal bank partially unveiled, in the absence of important witnesses, and in numerous charges confidently made and as yet wholly uninvestigated there was enough to induce a majority of the committee of investigation—a committee which was selected from the most able and honorable members of the House of Representatives—to recommend a suspension of further action upon the bill and a prosecution of the inquiry. As the charter had yet four years to run, and as a renewal now was not necessary to the successful prosecution of its business, it was to have been expected that the bank itself, conscious of its purity and proud of its character, would have withdrawn its application for the present, and demanded the severest scrutiny into all its transactions. In their declining to do so there seems to be an additional reason why the functionaries of the Government should proceed with less haste and more caution in the renewal of their monopoly. The bank is professedly established as an agent of the executive branch of the Government, and its constitutionality is maintained on that ground. Neither upon the propriety of present action nor upon the provisions of this act was the Executive consulted. It has had no opportunity to say that it neither needs nor wants an agent clothed with such powers and favored by such exemptions. There is nothing in its legitimate functions which makes it necessary or proper. Whatever interest or influence, whether public or private, has given birth to this act, it cannot be found either in the wishes or necessities of the executive department, by which present action is deemed premature, and the powers conferred upon its agent not only unnecessary, but dangerous to the Government and country.

It is to be regretted that the rich and powerful too often bend the acts of government to their selfish purposes. Distinctions in society will always exist under every just government. Equality of talents, of education, or of wealth cannot be produced by human institutions. In the full enjoyment of the gifts of Heaven and the fruits of superior industry, economy, and virtue, every man is equally entitled to protection by law; but when the laws undertake to add to these natural and just advantages artificial distinctions, to grant titles, gratuities, and exclusive privileges, to make the rich richer and the potent more powerful, the humble members of society-the farmers, mechanics, and laborers—who have neither the time nor the means of securing like favors to themselves, have a right to complain of the injustice of their Government. There are no necessary evils in government. Its evils exist only in its abuses. If it would confine itself to equal protection, and, as Heaven does its rains, shower its favors alike on the high and the low, the rich and the poor, it would be an unqualified blessing. In the act before me there seems to be a wide and unnecessary departure from these just principles. Nor is our Government to be maintained or our Union preserved by invasions of the rights and powers of the several States. In thus attempting to make our General Government strong we make it weak. Its true strength consists in leaving individuals and States as much as possible to themselves—in making itself felt, not in its power, but in its beneficence; not in its control, but in its protection; not in binding the States more closely to the center, but leaving each to move unobstructed in its proper orbit.

Experience should teach us wisdom. Most of the difficulties our Government now encounters and most of the dangers which impend over our Union have sprung from an abandonment of the legitimate objects of Government by our national legislation, and the adoption of such principles as are embodied in this act. Many of our rich men have not been content with equal protection and equal benefits, but have besought us to make them richer by act of Congress. By attempting to gratify their desires we have in the results of our legislation arrayed section against section, interest against interest, and man against man, in a fearful commotion which threatens to shake the foundations of our Union. It is time to pause in our career to review our principles, and if possible revive that devoted patriotism and spirit of compromise which distinguished the sages of the Revolution and the fathers of our Union. If we cannot at once, in justice to interests vested under improvident legislation, make our Government what it ought to be, we can at least take a stand against all new grants of monopolies and exclusive privileges, against any prostitution of our Government to the advancement of the few at the expense of the many, and in favor of compromise and gradual reform in our code of laws and system of political economy.

I have now done my duty to my country. If sustained by my fellow citizens, I shall be grateful and happy; if not, I shall find in the motives which impel me ample grounds for contentment and peace. In the difficulties which surround us and the dangers which threaten our institutions there is cause for neither dismay nor alarm. For relief and deliverance let us firmly rely on that kind Providence which I am sure watches with peculiar care over the destinies of our Republic, and on the intelligence and wisdom of our countrymen. Through His abundant goodness and heir patriotic devotion our liberty and Union will be preserved.

Andrew Jackson,
Washington, July 10, 1832[1]

Notes

CHAPTER 1. THE FORGOTTEN WAR OF 1812

1. Williams, *Legions of Satan.*
2. "Impressment of American Sailors," *The Mariners Museum,* www.mariners museum.org/sites/micro/usnavy/08/08a.htm (accessed March 12, 2016).
3. Kawa, "The Story behind the Most Insidious Rothschild Dynasty Conspiracy Theory," www.businessinsider.com/rothschild-family-war-of -1812-conspiracy-2013-1 (accessed March 12, 2016).
4. Foreman, "The British View the War of 1812 Quite Differently than Americans Do," www.smithsonianmag.com/history/british-view-war -1812-quite-differently-americans-do-180951852 (accessed March 12, 2016).
5. Jones, "Washington D.C. Hurricane of 1814," http://usforeignpolicy.about. com/od/introtoforeignpolicy/a/Washington-D-C-Hurricane-Of-1814.htm (accessed March 12, 2016).
6. Dodge, "Constitution Printed in 1825," www.lawfulpath.com/ref/13th -amend.shtml (accessed May 16, 2016).
7. Eggleston and Seelye, "A Speech by Tecumseh," 182–86.

CHAPTER 2.
THE ROTHSCHILDS WIN AGAIN (1815–1825)

1. "Rothschild Fortune," http://trove.nla.gov.au/ndp/del/article/1401561 (accessed March 12, 2016).
2. "Famous Quotations on Banking," www.themoneymasters.com/the-money -masters/famous-quotations-on-banking (accessed March 12, 2016).
3. Griffin, in "The Bank Was Saved and the People Were Ruined," www

.lewrockwell.com/2012/10/jeff-thomas/the-bank-was-saved-and-the-people -were-ruined (accessed March 12, 2016).

4. Knight, "Nicholas Biddle," http://what-when-how.com/conspiracy-theories -in-american-history/biddle-nicholas (accessed March 12, 2016).

5. "Return of the Debtors' Prison?" www.pbs.org/newshour/bb/return-debtors -prison (accessed March 12, 2016).

6. *History of Erie County, Volume 1,* www.examiner.com/article/the-giant -mound-builders-of-erie (accessed March 12, 2016).

7. Haywood, *The Natural and Aboriginal History of Tennessee,* https://archive .org/details/naturalaborigina00hayw (accessed March 12, 2016).

8. Barber, in *History and Antiquities of Every Connecticut Town,* www .barbar adelong.com/special-projects/giants/north-american-giants (accessed March 12, 2016).

9. Biddle, in Porton, *Life of Andrew Jackson,* 81–82, www.forgottenbooks .com/readbook_text/Life_of_Andrew_Jackson_v3_1000519122/81 (accessed March 12, 2014).

CHAPTER 3.
ANDREW JACKSON STEPS INTO
THE ARENA (1826–1831)

1. "Three Famous Duels Involving Andrew Jackson," http://hubpages.com/ hub/3-Famous-Duels-Involving-Andrew-Jackson (accessed March 12, 2016).

2. Wernecke, "My God! Have I Missed Him?" http://teachingamericanhistory .org/past-programs/hfotw/120528-2 (accessed March 12, 2016).

3. Bomboy, "The Story of the Wildest Party in White House History," http:// blog.constitutioncenter.org/2013/03/the-story-of-the-wildest-party-in-white -house-history (accessed March 12, 2016).

4. Turner, *History of the Pioneer Settlement of Phelps and Gorham's Purchase, and Morris' Reserve,* 428, https://books.google.com/books?id=TUX698v 8KGkC&printsec=frontcover&dq=History+of+the+Pioneer+Settlement +of+the+Phelps (accessed March 12, 2016).

5. Winfield, "Search for the Lost Giants (in WYN), Part 2," http://buffalorising .com/2015/02/the-search-for-the-lost-giants-in-wny-part-2 (accessed March 12, 2016).

6. Howe, in the *Spalding Research Project,* http://solomonspalding.com/SRP/ saga2/sagawt0a.htm (accessed March 12, 2016).

7. McGavin, in the *Spalding Research Project,* http://solomonspalding.com/ SRP/saga2/sagawt0a.htm (accessed March 12, 2016).

8. Marks, in the *Spalding Research Project,* http://solomonspalding.com/SRP/ saga2/sagawt0a.htm (accessed March 12, 2016).

9. *History of Erie County, Volume 1,* in Swope, "The Giant Mound Builders of Erie," http://solomonspalding.com/SRP/saga2/1884Eri1.htm (accessed March 12, 2016).

10. *Jefferson Gazette* of Ashtabula County, Ohio, in the *Spalding Research Project,* http://solomonspalding.com/SRP/saga2/sagawt0a.htm (accessed March 12, 2016).

CHAPTER 4.
BATTLING THE SEVEN-HEADED HYDRA (1832–1835)

1. Denslow, *10,000 Famous Freemasons,* in "Presidents That Were Brother Masons," http://jl1.org/join/u-s-presidents.html (accessed March 12, 2016).

2. "President Jackson's Veto Message," http://avalon.law.yale.edu/19th_century/ ajveto01.asp (accessed March 12, 2016).

3. Meacham, *American Lion,* 256.

4. "Roger B. Taney," *Wikipedia,* https://en.wikipedia.org/wiki/Roger_B._Taney (accessed March 12, 2016).

5. Remini, *Andrew Jackson: The Course of American Democracy, 1833–1845,* 108.

6. Draughton, *Financial Armageddon,* 87.

7. www.whitehouse.gov/1600/presidents/andrewjackson.

CHAPTER 5.
JACKSON KILLS THE BANK (1836–1846)

1. Boardman, *America and the Jacksonian Era 1825–1850,* 25.

2. Myers, *A Financial History of the United States,* 93.

3. McGrane, *Panic of 1837,* 65.

4. Timberlake, quoted in Rousseau, "Jacksonian Monetary Policy, Specie Flows and the Panic of 1837," 458, www.nber.org/papers/w7528 (accessed March 12, 2016).

5. McDougall, *Throes of Democracy,* 75–76.

6. Rousseau, "Jacksonian Monetary Policy," 479–80, www.nber.org/papers/ w7528 (accessed March 13, 2016).

7. Sumner, *Andrew Jackson,* 392–94.

8. McGrane, *Panic of 1837,* 97.

9. Rousseau, "Jacksonian Monetary Policy," 486–87, www.nber.org/papers/ w7528 (accessed March 13, 2016).

10. Whalen, *Inflated: How Money and Debt Built the American Dream,* 21.

11. Wilson, *History of the American People IV,* 66–72.

12. Karsner, *Andrew Jackson,* 386–87.

CHAPTER 6.
ANCIENT GIANTS AND WESTWARD EXPANSION
(1847–1857)

1. *The Middletown Signal,* in Graham, "Today's Giant Is from Miamisburg, Ohio," http://sherrycottlegraham.com/2013/11/23/todays-giant-is-from -miamisburg-oh (accessed March 12, 2016).

2. "A Giant Discovered," *Madison Banner, Niles' National Register,* https:// books.google.com/books?id=XHwFAAAAQAAJ&pg=PA70&lpg=PA70 &dq=We+are+informed (accessed March 12, 2016).

3. "Giant's Bones," Newspaper Accounts of Giants, www.jasoncolavito.com/ newspaper-accounts-of-giants.html (accessed March 12, 2016).

4. *New York Herald,* Newspaper Accounts of Giants, www.jasoncolavito.com/ newspaper-accounts-of-giants.html, accessed March 12, 2016.

5. http://quod.lib.umich.edu/1/lincoln/lincoln2//1:6?rgn=divl;view= fulltext

6. "Monsters from the Mound," Mason C. Winfield, January 15, 2001. www .xprojectmagazine.com/archives/strange/skeleton_mound.html.

7. "Skeleton of a Giant Found," *New York Times,* Newspaper Accounts of Giants, www.jasoncolavito.com/newspaper-accounts-of-giants.html (accessed March 12, 2016).

8. *Boston Medical Journal* reprinted story, Newspaper Accounts of Giants, www.jasoncolavito.com/newspaper-accounts-of-giants.html.

CHAPTER 7.
THE ROTHSCHILDS AND THE CIVIL WAR
(1858–1861)

1. "Race-Based Legislation in the North," www.pbs.org/wgbh/aia/part4/ 4p2957.html (accessed March 12, 2016).

2. Introduction to "Slavery in the North," http://slavenorth.com (accessed March 12, 2016).

3. "America's First Slave Owner Was a Black Man," http://conservative-headlines.com/2012/03/americas-first-slave-owner-was-a-black-man (accessed March 12, 2016).

4. Franklin, in Gates, "Did Black People Own Slaves?" www.theroot.com/articles/history/2013/03/black_slave_owners_did_they_exist.html (accessed March 12, 2016).

5. Ibid.

6. *Times of London*, in Griffin, "The Rothschilds and the Civil War," http://rense.com/general78/brudt.htm (accessed March 12, 2016).

7. Diamond, *A Casual View of America*, 4.

8. "Salomon James de Rothschild" *Wikipedia,* https://en.wikipedia.org/wiki/Salomon_James_de_Rothschild (accessed March 12, 2016).

9. "Salomon de Rothschild Tours America (1861)," www.theoccident.com/Salomon/salo16.html (accessed March 13, 2016).

10. "The Capitalist Cabal: 1830–1900," www.hermes-press.com/cabal_1830.htm (accessed March 13, 2016).

CHAPTER 8. ABRAHAM LINCOLN
DISCOVERS THE TRUTH (1862–1865)

1. *Money: A Monthly Magazine,* vols. 1–2, 4, https://books.google.com/books?id=5TgzAQAAMAAJ&pg=RA10-PA16&dq=We+gave+the+people+of+this+republic (accessed March 13, 2016).

2. Chaitkin, "Abraham Lincoln's Bank War," http://members.tripod.com/american_almanac/lincoln3.htm (accessed March 13, 2016).

3. Knuth, *Empire of the City,* 90.

4. Masur, "How the South Could Have Been Saved," www.salon.com/2015/04/11/how_the_south_could_have_been_saved_abraham_lincolns_last_speech_and_a_vision_unrealized (accessed March 13, 2016).

CHAPTER 9.
ASSASSIN'S CREED: JOHN WILKES BOOTH (1865–?)

1. Hill, "Recollections of Abraham Lincoln 1847–1865," 116–17, http://rogerjnorton.com/Lincoln46.html (accessed March 13, 2016).

2. McGowan, "Why Everything You Think You Know about the Lincoln Assassination Is Wrong, Part 9," www.futile.work/nwsltrs/why-everything-you-think-you-know-about-the-lincoln-assassination-is-wrong-part-9.

3. Winkler, *Lincoln and Booth,* 143.

4. Trex, "The Time John Wilkes Booth's Brother Saved Abe Lincoln's Son," http://mentalfloss.com/article/56482/time-john-wilkes-booths-brother-saved-abe-lincolns-son (accessed March 13, 2016).

5. McGowan, "Why Everything You Think You Know about the Lincoln Assassination Is Wrong, Part 10," www.futile.work/nwsltrs/why-everything-you-think-you-know-about-the-lincoln-assassination-is-wrong-part-10.

6. Ibid., Part 5, www.futile.work/nwsltrs/why-everything-you-think-you-know-about-the-lincoln-assassination-is-wrong-part-5.

7. Swanson, "The Final Hours of John Wilkes Booth," www.smithsonianmag.com/history/final-hours-john-wilkes-booth-180954853 (accessed March 13, 2016).

8. "John Wilkes Booth," *Unsolved Mysteries,* http://unsolved.com/archives/john-wilkes-booth (accessed March 13, 2016).

9. Ibid.

10. Ibid.

11. Ibid.

12. Ibid.

13. Ibid.

14. Meltzer and Ferrell, *History Decoded,* 16.

15. "John Wilkes Booth Mystery," *People and Family,* www.rootsweb.ancestry.com/~okgarftp/people/booth.htm (accessed March 13, 2016).

16. "The Secret Life of Jesse James," www.mackwhite.com/Bison8.html (accessed March 13, 2016).

17. "Outliers: Bones of Contention," www.modernhealthcare.com/article/20130817/MAGAZINE/308179967 (accessed March 13, 2016).

APPENDIX.
PRESIDENT JACKSON'S VETO MESSAGE REGARDING
THE BANK OF THE UNITED STATES (JULY 10, 1832)

1. "President Jackson's Veto Message," http://avalon.law.yale.edu/19th_century/ajveto01.asp (accessed March 13, 2016).

Bibliography

"A Giant Discovered." *Madison Banner, Niles' National Register* (October 4, 1845). https://books.google.com/books?id=XHwFAAAAQAAJ&pg=PA70&lpg= PA70&dq=We+are+informed. Accessed March 12, 2016.

"America's First Slave Owner Was a Black Man." *Conservative Headlines*. http:// conservative-headlines.com/2012/03/americas-first-slave-owner-was-a-black -man. Accessed March 12, 2016.

Barber, John Warner. *History and Antiquities of Every Connecticut Town*. Hartford, Conn.: A. Willard, 1836. Quoted in "North American Giants." www .barbaradelong.com/special-projects/giants/north-american-giants. Accessed March 12, 2016.

Biddle, Nicholas. Quoted in Porton, *Life of Andrew Jackson*. www.forgotten books.com/readbook_text/Life_of_Andrew_Jackson_v3_1000519122/81. Accessed March 12, 2016.

Boardman, Fon Wyman. *America and the Jacksonian Era 1825–1850*. New York: H. Z. Walck, 1975.

Bomboy, Scott. "The Story of the Wildest Party in White House History." *Constitution Daily* (March 4, 2013). http://blog.constitutioncenter .org/2013/03/the-story-of-the-wildest-party-in-white-house-history. Accessed March 12, 2016.

Boston Medical Journal reprint of a story in the Burlington, Iowa, *State Gazette*. www.jasoncolavito.com/newspaper-accounts-of-giants.html. Accessed March 12, 2016.

"The Capitalist Cabal: 1830–1900." www.hermespress.com/cabal_1830.htm. Accessed March 13, 2016.

Chaitkin, Anton. "Abraham Lincoln's Bank War." *Executive Intelligence Review*

(May 30, 1986). http://members.tripod.com/american_almanac/lincoln .htm. Accessed March 13, 2016.

Denslow, William R. *10,000 Famous Freemasons*. Independence, Mo.: Missouri Lodge of Research, 1957. In "Presidents That Were Brother Masons." Jackson Lodge #1 F. & A.M. http://jl1.org/join/u-s-presidents.html. Accessed March 12, 2016.

Diamond, Sigmund. *A Casual View of America: The Home Letters of Salomon de Rothschild 1859–1861*. London: The Cresset Press, 1962.

Dodge, David. "Constitution Printed in 1825." *The Lawful Path* (August 1, 1991). www.lawfulpath.com/ref/13th-amend.shtml. Accessed May 16, 2016.

Draughton, David B. *Financial Armageddon: The Corruption of our Currency*. Spring Hill, Utah: 2007.

Eggleston, Edward, and L. E. Seelye. "A Speech by Tecumseh." *Tecumseh and the Shawnee Prophet*. New York: Dodd, Mead and Co., 1878. http://faculty .humanities.uci.edu/tcthorne/Hist15/tecumseh1811.html. Accessed March 13, 2016.

"Famous Quotations on Banking." www.themoneymasters.com/the-money -masters/famous-quotations-on-banking. Accessed March 12, 2016.

Foreman, Amanda. "The British View the War of 1812 Quite Differently Than Americans Do." *Smithsonian Magazine* (July 2014). www.smithsonianmag .com/history/british-view-war-1812-quite-differently-americans-do -180951852. Accessed March 12, 2016.

Franklin, John Hope. Quoted in Gates, Henry Louis Jr. "Did Black People Own Slaves?" *The Root* (March 4, 2013). www.theroot.com/articles/history/ 2013/03/black_slave_owners_did_they_exist.html. Accessed March 12, 2016.

"Giant's Bones." *Western Weekly Review*. (Franklin, Tenn.: November 11, 1845). Newspaper Accounts of Giants. www.jasoncolavito.com/newspaper-accounts -of-giants.html. Accessed March 12, 2016.

Graham, Sherry Cottle. "Today's Giant Is from Miamisburg, Ohio." *Mound Builder Children, the "Historical Collections of Ohio, 1848*. R977.1–H83. Miamisburg Public LibraryMiamisburg, Ohio. http://sherrycottlegraham .com/2013/11/23/todays-giant-is-from-miamisburg-oh. Accessed March 12, 2016.

Griffin, Des. "The Rothschilds and the Civil War." *Descent into Slavery*. Clackamas, Ore.: Emissary Publications, 2001. http://rense.com/general78/ brudt.htm. Accessed March 12, 2016.

Griffin, G. Edward, in "The Bank Was Saved and the People Were Ruined" by Jeff Thomas. (October 10, 2012). www.lewrockwell.com/2012/10/jeff-thomas/the-bank-was-saved-and-the-people-were-ruined. Accessed March 12, 2016.

Haywood, John. *The Natural and Aboriginal History of Tennessee.* Nashville, Tenn.: George Wilson, 1823. https://archive.org/details/naturalaborigina00hayw. Accessed March 12, 2016.

Hill, Lamon Ward. "Recollections of Abraham Lincoln 1847–1865." Lincoln: University of Nebraska Press, 1994. http://rogerjnorton.com/Lincoln46.html. Accessed March 13, 2016.

History of Erie County, Volume 1, www.examiner.com/article/the-giant-mound-builders-of-erie. Accessed March 12, 2016.

———. Quoted in Robin Swope, "The Giant Mound Builders of Erie." *Examiner* (July 5, 2010). http://solomonspalding.com/SRP/saga2/1884Eri1.htm. Accessed March 12, 2016.

Howe, Henry. *Historical Collections of Ohio,* in "The Conneaut Giants." *The Spalding Research Project.* http://solomonspalding.com/SRP/saga2/sagawt0a.htm. Accessed March 12, 2016.

"Monsters from the Mound," Mason C. Winfield, January 15, 2001. *Paranormal Magazine.* www.xprojectmagazine.com/archives/strange/skeleton_mound.html.

"Impressment of American Sailors: Prelude to the War of 1812." *The Mariners Museum.* www.marinersmuseum.org/sites/micro/usnavy/08/08a.htm. Accessed March 12, 2016.

Jefferson Gazette of Ashtabula County, Ohio, in "The Conneaut Giants." *The Spalding Research Project.* http://solomonspalding.com/SRP/saga2/sagawt0a.htm. Accessed March 12, 2016.

"John Wilkes Booth." *Unsolved Mysteries.* http://unsolved.com/archives/john-wilkes-booth. Accessed March 13, 2016.

"John Wilkes Booth Mystery." *People and Family.* Garfield County Administrator. www.rootsweb.ancestry.com/~okgarftp/people/booth.htm. Accessed March 13, 2016.

Jones, Steve. "Washington D.C. Hurricane of 1814." *About News.* http://usforeignpolicy.about.com/od/introtoforeignpolicy/a/Washington-D-C-Hurricane. Accessed March 12, 2016.

Karsner, David. *Andrew Jackson: The Gentle Savage.* New York: Brentano's, 1929.

Kawa, Lucas. "The Story behind the Most Insidious Rothschild Dynasty Conspiracy Theory." *Business Insider* (January 8, 2013). www.businessinsider.com/rothschild-family-war-of-1812-conspiracy-2013–1. Accessed March 12, 2016.

Knight, Peter, ed. "Nicholas Biddle." *Conspiracy Theories in American History: An Encyclopedia.* http://what-when-how.com/conspiracy-theories-in-american-history/biddle-nicholas. Accessed March 12, 2016.

Knuth, Edwin C. *Empire of the City.* Milwaukee, Wisc.: Knuth, 1946.

Marks, David. "The Conneaut Giants." *The Spalding Research Project.* http://solomonspalding.com/SRP/saga2/sagawt0a.htm. Accessed March 12, 2016.

Masur, Louis P. "How the South Could Have Been Saved: Abraham Lincoln's Last Speech, and a Vision Unrealized." *Salon* (April 11, 2015). www.salon.com/2015/04/11/how_the_south_could_have_been_saved_abraham_lincolns_last_speech_and_a_vision_unrealized. Accessed March 13, 2016.

McDougall, Walter A. *Throes of Democracy: The American Civil War Era, 1829–1877.* New York: Harper, 2009.

McGavin, E. Cecil. *Geography of the Book of Mormon,* in "The Conneaut Giants." The Spalding Research Project. http://solomonspalding.com/SRP/saga2/sagawt0a.htm. Accessed March 12, 2016.

McGowan, Dave. "Why Everything You Think You Know about the Lincoln Assassination Is Wrong, Part 5." The Center for an Informed America (April 19, 2014). www.futile.work/nwsltrs/why-everything-you-think-you-know-about-the-lincoln-assassination-is-wrong-part-5.

———. "Why Everything You Think You Know about the Lincoln Assassination Is Wrong, Part 9." The Center for an Informed America (October 21, 2014). www.futile.work/nwsltrs/why-everything-you-think-you-know-about-the-lincoln-assassination-is-wrong-part-9.

———. "Why Everything You Think You Know about the Lincoln Assassination Is Wrong, Part 10." The Center for an Informed America (November 24, 2014). www.futile.work/nwsltrs/why-everything-you-think-you-know-about-the-lincoln-assassination-is-wrong-part-10.

McGrane, Reginald Charles. *Panic of 1837.* New York: Russell & Russell, Inc., 1965.

Meacham, Jon. *American Lion: Andrew Jackson in the White House.* New York: Random House, 2008.

Meltzer, Brad, and Keith Ferrell. *History Decoded: Solving the Ten Greatest Conspiracies of All Time.* New York: Workman Publishing Co., 2013.

Money: A Monthly Magazine, vols. 1–2, 4. New York: The Money Publishing Company, 1898. https://books.google.com/books?id=5TgzAQAAMAAJ &pg=RA1PA16&dq=We+gave+the+people+of+this+republic. Accessed March 13, 2016.

Myers, Margaret G. *A Financial History of the United States.* New York: Columbia University Press, 1970.

New York Herald article. Newspaper Accounts of Giants. www.jasoncolavito.com/ newspaper-accounts-of-giants.html. Accessed March 13, 2016.

"Outliers: Bones of Contention Key to John Wilkes Booth Mystery." *Modern Healthcare.* (August 17, 2013). www.modernhealthcare.com/article/20130817/ MAGAZINE/308179967. Accessed March 13, 2016.

Porton, James. *Life of Andrew Jackson.* London: Forgotten Books, 2013.

"President Jackson's Veto Message." Yale Law School, The Avalon Project. http://avalon.law.yale.edu/19th_century/ajveto01.asp. Accessed March 13, 2016.

"Race-Based Legislation in the North." *Africans in America,* PBS. www.pbs.org/ wgbh/aia/part4/4p2957.html. Accessed March 12, 2016.

Remini, Robert V. *Andrew Jackson: The Course of American Democracy, 1833–1845.* New York, Johns Hopkins University Press, 1998.

"Return of the Debtors' Prison? Many Jailed for the Inability to Pay Fines." *PBS Newshour* (December 28, 2014). www.pbs.org/newshour/bb/return-debtors -prison. Accessed March 12, 2016.

"Roger B. Taney." http://en.wikipedia.org/wiki/Roger_B._Taney.

"Rothschild Fortune." *Trove Digitized Newspapers* (July 13, 1918). http://trove .nla.gov.au/ndp/del/article/1401561. Accessed March 12, 2016.

Rousseau, Peter L. "Jacksonian Monetary Policy, Specie Flows and the Panic of 1837." *The Journal of Economic History* (June 2002): 458. www.nber.org/ papers/w7528. Accessed March 13, 2016.

"Salomon de Rothschild Tours America (1861)." www.theoccident.com/Salomon/ salo16.html. Accessed March 13, 2016.

"Salomon James de Rothschild." http://en.wikipedia.org/wiki/Salomon_James _de_Rothschild. Accessed March 12, 2016.

Schrader, Del, and Jesse James III. *Jesse James Was One of His Names.* Arcadia, Calif.: Santa Anita Press, 1975.

"Secret Life of Jesse James." www.mackwhite.com/Bison8.html. Accessed March 13, 2016.

"Skeleton of a Giant Found," *New York Times* (November 21, 1856). Newspaper Accounts of Giants. www.jasoncolavito.com/newspaper-accounts-of-giants .html. Accessed March 12, 2016.

"Slavery in the North." http://slavenorth.com. Accessed March 13, 2016.

Sumner, William Graham. *Andrew Jackson.* Boston and New York: Houghton Mifflin Company, 1899.

Swanson, James L. "The Final Hours of John Wilkes Booth." *Smithsonian Magazine* (April 8, 2015). www.smithsonianmag.com/history/final-hours -john-wilkes-booth-180954853. Accessed March 13, 2016.

Swope, Robin. "The Giant Mound Builders of Erie." *Examiner* (July 5, 2010). www.examiner.com/article/the-giant-mound-builders-of-erie. Accessed March 12, 2016.

"Three Famous Duels Involving Andrew Jackson." http://hubpages.com/hub/ 3-Famous-Duels-Involving-Andrew-Jackson. Accessed March 12, 2016.

Timberlake Jr., Richard H. Quoted in Rousseau, "Jacksonian Monetary Policy, Specie Flows and the Panic of 1837." www.nber.org/papers/w7528. Accessed March 12, 2016.

Trex, Ethan. "The Time John Wilkes Booth's Brother Saved Abe Lincoln's Son." *Mentalfloss.com* (April 30, 2014). http://mentalfloss.com/article/56482/time -john-wilkes-booths-brother-saved-abe-lincolns-son. Accessed March 13, 2016.

Turner, Orsamus. *History of the Pioneer Settlement of Phelps and Gorham's Purchase, and Morris' Reserve.* Rochester, N.Y.: William Alling, 1851. https:// books.google.com/books?id=TUX698v8KGkC&printsec=frontcover&dq= History+of+the+Pioneer+Settlement+of+the+Phelps. Accessed March 12, 2016.

Wernecke, Dantan. "My God! Have I Missed Him?" TeachingAmericanhistory .org (May 27, 2012). http://teachingamericanhistory.org/past-programs/ hfotw/120528-2. Accessed March 12, 2016.

Whalen, Christopher. *Inflated: How Money and Debt Built the American Dream.* Hoboken, N.J.: John Wiley and Sons, Inc., 2011.

Williams, Jonathan. *Legions of Satan.* London: N.p., 1781.

Wilson, Woodrow. *History of the American People IV: Critical Changes and Civil War.* New York: Harper and Brothers, 1902.

Winfield, Mason. "Search for the Lost Giants (in WYN), Part 2." Buffalorising
.com (February 15, 2015). http://buffalorising.com/2015/02/the-search
-for-the-lost-giants-in-wny-part-2. Accessed March 12, 2016.

Winkler, H. Donald. *Lincoln and Booth*. New York: Cumberland House,
2003.

Index

Page numbers in *italics* indicate illustrations

BOOKS OF RELATED INTEREST

The Suppressed History of America
The Murder of Meriwether Lewis and the Mysterious
Discoveries of the Lewis and Clark Expedition
by Paul Schrag and Xaviant Haze
Foreword by Michael Tsarion

Aliens in Ancient Egypt
The Brotherhood of the Serpent and the
Secrets of the Nile Civilization
by Xaviant Haze

The Ancient Giants Who Ruled America
The Missing Skeletons and the Great Smithsonian Cover-Up
by Richard J. Dewhurst

Advanced Civilizations of Prehistoric America
The Lost Kingdoms of the Adena, Hopewell,
Mississippians, and Anasazi
by Frank Joseph

Lost Race of the Giants
The Mystery of Their Culture, Influence, and
Decline throughout the World
by Patrick Chouinard

Founding Fathers, Secret Societies
Freemasons, Illuminati, Rosicrucians, and the
Decoding of the Great Seal
by Robert Hieronimus, Ph.D., with Laura Cortner

Templar Sanctuaries in North America
Sacred Bloodlines and Secret Treasures
by William F. Mann
Foreword by Scott F. Wolter

America: Nation of the Goddess
The Venus Families and the Founding of the United States
by Alan Butler and Janet Wolter
Foreword by Scott F. Wolter

INNER TRADITIONS • BEAR & COMPANY
P.O. Box 388 • Rochester, VT 05767 • 1-800-246-8648
www.InnerTraditions.com
Or contact your local bookseller